SIGNS (IN THE) HEAVENS

Unless otherwise indicated,
all Scripture quotations are taken from
the *King James Version* of the Bible.

ISBN 1-56441-016-1

Printed in the United States of America

SIGNS (IN THE) HEAVENS

Marilyn Hickey

Marilyn Hickey Ministries
P.O. Box 17340
Denver, Colorado 80217

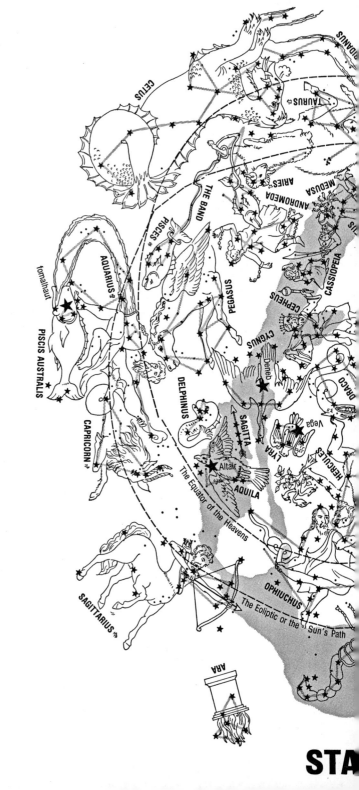

TAURUS

ERIDANUS

CETUS

THE BAND

PISCES

ARIES

ANDROMEDA

MEDUSA

CASSIOPEIA

PERSEUS

AQUARIUS ♒

fomalhaut

PISCIS AUSTRALIS

PEGASUS

CEPHEUS

CYGNUS

Deneb

DRACO

CAPRICORN ♑

DELPHINUS

SAGITTA

LYRA

Vega

HERCULES

The Equator of the Heavens

Altair

AQUILA

SAGITTARIUS ♐

OPHIUCHUS

The Ecliptic or the Sun's Path

ARA

STA

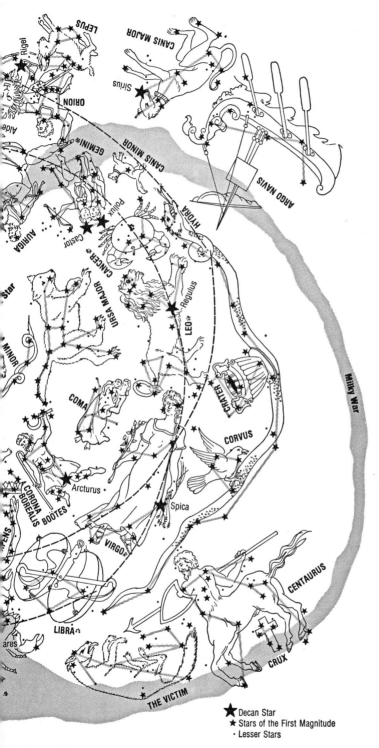

LEPUS

CANIS MAJOR

Rigel

ORION

Sirius

ARGO NAVIS

Alde

GEMINI

CANIS MINOR

Pollux

Castor

AURIGA

CANCER

HYDRA

Star

URSA MAJOR

LEO

Regulus

CRATER

COMA

MINOR

CORVUS

Arcturus

CORONA BOREALIS

BOOTES

Spica

SERENS

VIRGO

CENTAURUS

LIBRA

CRUX

ares

THE VICTIM

Milky War

★ Decan Star
★ Stars of the First Magnitude
· Lesser Stars

CHART

Contents

INTRODUCTION
WHAT SIGNS ARE IN THE HEAVENS?

Were you ever involved in reading your horoscope, studying astrology, or trying to predict your future by the stars? If you were, then you're not alone. Throughout the ages, the stars have provided a great source of fascination for millions of people! The devil has deceived people for thousands of years through astrology; he's convinced them that they could find answers to their questions about the future. Instead of seeking God for His wisdom, people have accepted one of Satan's greatest counterfeits: the lie of astrology.

For a long time I wondered how so many intelligent people could believe that they can know what's going to happen in their personal lives by seeing an answer in the stars of the heavens. But then I realized that "if Satan has gone to such great lengths to deceive people with his elaborate plan, he must be disguising a message that is for Christians!" I asked the Lord, "Do you have a special message for **us** in the stars?"

The purpose of this book is to give you knowledge of the miraculous story of redemption which God placed in the heavens for all to see. I want to share the discoveries which I have made through God's Word, and from studying the stars and the signs that **He placed** in the heavens.

When I began to study the Scriptures on this subject, the few people whom I mentioned my search to had a common response: "You're not getting involved in the occult, are you!" If you have any such fears, put them aside. I'm not dabbling with the occult; rather, my conclusions are based solely on God's Word, to uncover His divine plan as it was originally in the heavens.

As Christians, we ought to be aware of the revelation of the heavens which comes through God's Word. His Word gives us truth about the "controversial" subject of astrology—and it is our weapon that will beat the devil at his own game!

Let me start off by issuing the same warning that is set forth in the Bible about worship of the stars. God has specifically commanded us not to predict our futures through the stars! The reason God placed stars and planets in the heavens was to reveal knowledge about His Son, Jesus Christ. The Gospel of Matthew tells a beautiful story about the wise men who followed one radiant star on a long journey—and that star led them to their Savior. The Gospel says that the wise men followed "His star;" it actually belonged to Him! When the men saw the star they didn't say, "Who will I marry?" They didn't ask, "How many children will I have?" or "When will I die?" No!

It is important to realize that the star which these men followed did not lead them to ask questions about themselves! They knew from studying the heavens Who they would find: the Messiah, Jesus Christ. When they found Him, they worshiped Him; I believe that the Bible calls them **wise men** because they had seen God's plan of salvation through revelation in the stars.

If this study causes us to see what the heavens say about Jesus, and it causes us to worship Him, what will we be? **Wise** men and women! Keep in mind that this entire study is centered around the Lord Jesus Christ, and Him alone.

Today, there is a growing awareness of the impending return of Jesus, and His final judgment upon the earth. Prophecy records warnings of signs which will herald Jesus' return, and God would not have set forth those prophecies if He didn't want us to be aware of His plan! He spoke of many signs in the heavens in relation to Jesus' return:

> "And there shall be signs in the sun, and in
> the moon, and in the stars; and upon the

earth distress of nations, with perplexity; the
sea and the waves roaring; Men's hearts
failing them for fear, and for looking after
those things which are coming on the earth:
for the powers of heaven shall be shaken. And
then shall they see the Son of man coming in
a cloud with power and great glory" (Luke
21:25-27).

Where does that Scripture say that the signs of Jesus'
return will be? In the heavens! Right where God placed them
from the beginning of time. Jesus prophesied that we would
see signs in the heavens and said that we would **know** that
His return was near.

Increasing numbers of people have claimed that we are
actually living in the "last days" of God's dispensation of
grace before His. judgment; and most Bible scholars are in
agreement with that point. How can people be sure that
Christ will soon remove believers from the earth in what is
called "the Rapture?" Jesus Himself said:

"For then shall be great tribulation, such as
was not since the beginning of the world to
this time, no, nor ever shall be. And except
those days should be shortened, there should
no flesh be saved:. . ." (Matthew 24:21,22).

Jesus prophesied changes in the sun, the moon, and the
stars. His prophetic words are now being confirmed frequently by scientists. They are predicting that days will shorten in
length, the earth's axis will alter, that the earth will undergo
famines, pestilences, earthquakes, and increased volcanic activity; and they are also saying that the sun's activity will
disrupt the earth's ionosphere, communications systems,
wind directions, rainfall, and temperatures. I find it in-

11

teresting to note that the world's "geniuses" are only confirming what God set forth approximately two thousand years ago—that Jesus is returning to catch His Church away into glory!

Jesus, however, is not the only One Who directs our attention to the heavens concerning the "last days." John, the revelator, spoke this inspiration by the Spirit of God:

> "And the fourth angel sounded, and the third
> part of the sun was smitten, and the third part
> of the moon, and the third part of the stars; so
> as the third part of them was darkened, and
> the day shone not for a third part of it, and
> the night likewise" (Revelation 8:12).

What happened? The length of daylight was shortened by one-third! Before the flood, which is described in the book of Genesis in chapter seven, the earth was not watered by rainfall, but by mists arising from the waters of the earth. The great flood shook things up so drastically that the fountains of the deep were broken up, and rain and snow became the earth's source of water. At this time, the earth's axis was altered by **23 degrees.**

Compare the lengths of man's lifespans before and after the flood. Before the flood, man's average lifespan was much longer than it is now. You will find that the signs in the heavens will not only have great effects on the earth's activity—they will even alter the lengths of men's lives. All of these events are what will point to our living hope: Jesus.

In Matthew 24:7, Jesus prophesied:

> "For nation shall rise against nation, and
> kingdom against kingdom: and there shall be
> famines and pestilences, and earthquakes, in
> divers places."

This verse sounds as though it was quoted from today's newspaper! Nations **are** rising up in war against each other; all over the earth, tremendous famines are occurring because of drought and weather changes. There have also been devastating earthquakes. In the past century, there have been more earthquakes recorded than in all of history. The volcanoes which have "slept" for thousands of years have been recently erupting—darkening the skies, and shortening the days!

How are we supposed to react to all of these signs of Jesus' coming? You'll find the answer in II Peter 3:11,12:

> "Seeing then that all these things shall be dissolved, what manner of persons ought ye to be in all holy conversation and godliness, Looking for and hasting unto the coming of the day of God, wherein the heavens being on fire shall be dissolved, and the elements shall melt with fervent heat?"

I'd say that, since the heavens will dissolve with fire, and the elements will melt with fervent heat, that's a pretty good reason for us to keep ourselves "in all holy conversation and godliness!" Peter was saying, "Stay holy, and look forward to Jesus' return!" That's the type of behavior that a Christian ought to maintain. The Christian ought to be looking ahead to the day when we'll be caught up "in the twinkling of an eye" (I Cor. 15:52). While the world may look ahead and see only tribulation—we can see **translation!**

God has told us what He plans to do in the future so that we aren't taken by surprise. Because He wants us to be watching for Jesus' return and keeping ourselves holy, we can understand that His prophetic warnings are given in advance because of His great love and mercy for us. But the love and mercy of God are magnified even more greatly when we can realize that He has written a message of His plan in the stars! The very first chapter of Genesis states why God placed stars in the heavens:

> "And God said, Let there be lights in the firmament of the heaven to divide the day from the night; and **let them be for signs,** and for seasons, and for days, and years" (Genesis 1:14).

The planets and stars which shine brightly at night were placed in the heavens not only to give you light, but also to be signs of God's plan. They are to lead you to the worship of Jesus Christ, not to help you predict your future. Numbers 24:17 even prophesied about the star which would lead the wise men to Jesus Christ:

> "I shall see him, but not now: I shall behold him, but not nigh: there shall come a star out of Jacob, and a Sceptre shall rise out of Israel, and shall smite the corners of Moab, and destroy all the children of Sheth" (Numbers 24:17).

Who was the Sceptre of Israel? He is Jesus, the One to Whom the stars will lead you. David wrote a psalm which reveals why God placed signs in the heavens:

> "The heavens declare the glory of God; and the firmament sheweth his handywork. Day unto day uttereth speech, and night unto night sheweth knowlege" (Psalm 19:1,2).

Every night, when the light of the sun is reflected upon the planets, and the stars are visible, they shine forth the knowledge of God! Do you want to see how God revealed signs of His perfect plan in heavens? Discover what I discovered: that the heavens truly do declare the glory of God; see how His plan unfolds from beginning to end, and how it is still being confirmed. You don't need to fear your future or seek answers from the signs in the heavens. Instead, discover how Jesus' life is therein set forth—even telling of your own salvation and His soon return!

WHY GOD NAMED THE STARS

The book of Genesis clearly defines what God created during the six days of active creation (He rested on the seventh day). The first knowledge which the Bible sets out about the stars is to tell us **what** they are for, and also specify the fact that God Himself did create them:

> "And God said, Let there be lights in the firmament of the heaven to divide the day from the night; and let them be for signs, and for seasons, and for days, and years: And let them be for lights in the firmament of the heaven to give light upon the earth: and it was so. And God made two great lights; the greater light to rule the day, and the lesser light to rule the night: he made the stars also" (Genesis 1:14-16).

God created the stars, and then He proceeded to name and number every one of them! Psalm 147:4 verifies this, "He telleth the number of the stars; He calleth them all by their names." For what reason did God name the stars? You will discover that many of their names are significant in revealing the events of Jesus' birth, life, resurrection and return. The names of the stars are a very important detail of God's truth in the heavens.

I am convinced that God desires His people to focus their attention on what the heavens themselves declare. He has set forth a truth which no man, no demon in hell, and no angel can alter: **it is the story of Jesus Christ, and of His finished work, your redemption.**

Before you begin seeing exactly how God has revealed His plan to you through signs in the heavens, I want to address any desires of readers to continue using horoscopes for guidance and revelation. It is true that many people have seen "validity" in horoscopes, but that is only because Satan will mimic the truth whenever possible. Although many people don't accept astrology, at the same time, they will not totally reject it. You must realize that astrology is not from God; it is from the devil. I want you to make a decision according to God's Word and not involve yourself with astrology ever again, so I will share one woman's testimony. She is a born again Christian who once wrote articles for magazines as an astrologer—she **knows** about the temptation to continue with "minor" involvement in the devil's devices:

When she became a Christian, she gave up astrology with great reluctance. She was still haunted by her old desires, so she prayed intensively about the matter. Scripture stated that astrology was associated with the occult, and was an abomination to the Lord (Daniel 1:20, 2:2, 2:27, 4:7, 5:11; Deuteronomy 18:9-14). But she couldn't help but wonder why she had to completely cut off any involvement in astrology; after all, she'd seen it work in people's lives many times!

Was the **misuse** of astrology wrong? Or was it wrong to be involved in it at all? She praised God that He revealed this truth to she: Satan uses all of his power to blind men from seeing Christ's light. He only wants to "reveal" future events to astrologers, and even manipulate events to bring them to pass, because it gets people's eyes off Christ. Then, when people are deceived by one or two tricks, the impression they have is that "they have found the truth." That is stupid! The surprising part is that it takes so little to deceive most people—yet they expect tons and tons of evidence before they will accept the truth of God's Word!

Horoscope involvement even exerts its control over the lives of uninformed Christians. Believers must take a stand that says "I'm totally against astrology;" there's no such thing

17

as "riding the fence." I knew a man who had his horoscope read for the purpose of exposing astrology as a hoax. To his amazement, both good and bad predicitions started coming to pass! When he realized his mistake as sin, and repented before the Lord, the remainder of "unfulfilled" horoscope predictions failed to materialize, because the man had broken Satan's power and returned to the protection of God's authority.

Astrology is Satan's big lie which he used to keep men from understanding the way of salvation. At the cross, Christ has already triumphed over Satan, and He gives Christians the authority to live above every element in the spirit world. Don't be deceived into seeking answers from the stars. Instead, seek answers from the One Who created them.

Job was a wise man who studied the stars, and historians report that the book of Job is one of the oldest books of the Bible. It is a tremendous book for its day, filled with vast amounts of knowledge about God. Where could Job have acquired his knowledge? How could he know so much about God? I used to find myself wondering about these questions, because Job's revelation of God was not perceived through written material; and there were no prophets to tell him about God, either. But the book of Job has more to say about the stars than any other book of the Bible. I believe that God unfolded His truth to Job within the heavens, themselves!

Amazingly, Job even knew about the Messiah Who God would send thousands of years later; he said, "I know that my Redeemer liveth" (Job 19:25). Job never worshiped the stars or tried to predict his future through studying them. Instead, he let them lead him to Jesus.

If you have been reading this book, and you have had an interest (either passive or active) in astrology, or if you're looking to see how your "sign" depicts your future—forget it! The word **zodiac** is taken from the Greek word **zoad,** meaning "a ladder" or "steps;" and the great story in the stars is a "ladder" which leads men to the knowledge of their Savior.

A born again believer can now consider himself to be under "the sign of the cross." If anyone ever asks you "your sign," be bold and tell them that you've been marked by the Name above every name and that your identification is with Jesus Christ. Then, share with them about how they can receive Jesus' sign—the cross.

Christians, wanting to obey God's command to not worship the stars, have virtually ignored the signs in the heavens. But today, let this "zodiac," or "heavenly stepladder" reveal God's plan for His Son in your life. Just as the wise men followed Jesus' star at His birth, and worshiped Him, you can be wise today as you see God's Son as "the Way" to salvation and to the Father.

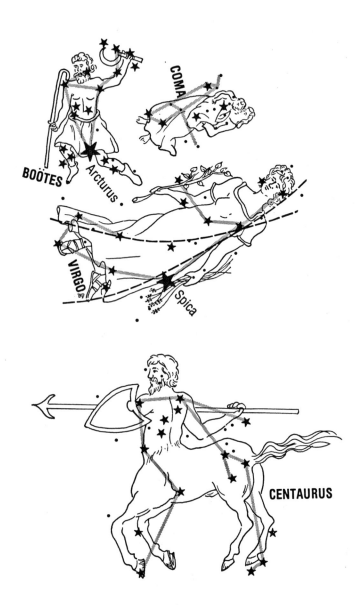

BOÖTES

COMA

Arcturus

VIRGO

Spica

CENTAURUS

CHAPTER ONE

VIRGO

Astrologers say that **Aquarius** is the first sign in the Zodiac—but this is just another aspect of Satan's counterfeit! The Zodiac chart actually begins with a different "sign." (Remember, **Zodiac** really means "a ladder," or "steps.") According to God's plan, the first rung of the ladder which points to Jesus is the sign of Virgo. Why? Because the word **Virgo** really means "virgin," and relates directly to Jesus' virgin birth.

Since ancient times, four symbols have been associated with Virgo. They are:

1. Virgo, the virgin;
2. Coma, a woman holding a baby;
3. Centaurus, the centaur, who is a half-man and half-horse creature; and
4. Bootes, a shepherd, or harvester.

The figure of Virgo holds a sheaf of wheat in her left hand, and within it is the constellation's brightest star called **Spica,** which means "seed." After Adam's fall, God told Satan:

> "And I will put enmity between thee and the woman, and between thy seed and her seed; it shall bruise thy head, and thou shalt bruise his heel" (Genesis 3:15).

Who is this prophecy referring to? It is about Jesus Christ, born of a virgin, and called "the Seed of woman!" The woman does not normally carry the seed (or sperm), of course—it is always the man who carries it. In this case, we see that God, through the Holy Spirit, is the Father by supernatural means. Isaiah 7:14 sheds some light on this first prophecy:

> "Therefore the Lord himself shall give you a sign; Behold, a virgin shall conceive, and bear a son, and shall call his name Immanuel."

> ". . .Joseph, son of David, do not be afraid to take Mary as your wife; for that which has been conceived in her is of the Holy Spirit. And she will bear a son; and you shall call his name Jesus, for it is He who will save His people from their sins" (Matthew 1:20, 21 NAS).

God magnified the importance of this "Seed" for all men to see: **Spica** is the brightest star in the constellation of Virgo. The "enmity" which God placed between Satan and woman was our Redeemer, the "Seed of woman," Jesus Christ!

> "And the dragon was enraged with the woman, and went off to make war with the rest of her offspring, who keep the commandments of God and hold to the testimony of Jesus" (Revelation 12:17, NAS).

This constellation brings the promise of a coming Messiah, praise the Lord! In Virgo's hand is a branch, upon which is a smaller star called **Subilon**—which means "Branch." The Lord gave us many Scriptures about Jesus as "the Branch." One of them is Isaiah 11:1:

"And there shall come forth a rod out of the stem of Jesse, and a Branch shall grow out of his roots:. . . ."

The prophet Zechariah prophesied that Jesus would be "the Branch," in two Scriptures: 1) ". . .I will bring forth my servant the Branch (Zechariah 3:8); and 2) ". . .Behold the man whose name is The Branch;. . .He shall build the temple of the Lord" (Zechariah 6:12).

The prophet Jeremiah also prophesied about Jesus as "the Branch":

"Behold, the days come, saith the Lord, that I will raise unto David a righteous Branch, and a King shall reign and prosper, and shall execute judgment and justice in the earth" (Jeremiah 23:5).

These prophecies present a thrilling picture of the Seed of woman Who was born of the lineage of David. He became the "Branch"—the right hand Man of His Father, Who was sent to us to secure our salvation.

Now look at the second figure in this constellation: a woman who is holding a baby, symbolizing the virgin Mary and the Baby Jesus. It contains a star named **Coma,** positioned upon the Baby. This star has a beautiful meaning: "The Desired One." Jesus, the long hoped-for Messiah, is the Desired One:

"And I will shake all nations, and the desire of all nations shall come: and I will fill this house with glory, saith the Lord of hosts" (Haggai 2:7).

Malachi 3:1 tells us the effect that the Desired One has

upon His people: "...and the Lord, whom ye seek...even the messenger of the covenant, whom ye **delight in:** behold, he shall come, saith the Lord of Hosts." God was saying very plainly that the "Desire of Nations," Jesus Christ, was One Whom we would take great delight in! If Jesus, in His Godly perfection, were presented as He truly is—He would be irresistible!

The third figure which is associated with the constellation of Virgo is a Shepherd named from ancient star maps, **Bootes.** The Scriptures frequently refer to Jesus as the Good Shepherd, and that is exactly Who this star represents. He is prophesied of in Isaiah 40:11, which says that "He shall feed his flock like a shepherd: he shall gather the lambs with his arm, and carry them in his bosom, and shall gently lead those that are with young."

In the New Testament, I Peter 2:25 calls Jesus the "Shepherd and Bishop of your souls." Jesus Himself said, "**I am** the good shepherd and know my sheep, and am known of mine" (John 10:14).

It is very interesting that the "Bo" of Bootes means "the coming One." John the Baptist knew that he was only the Messiah's forerunner. He referred to Jesus in John 1:26-27, saying, "...but there standeth one among you, whom ye know not; He it is, who coming after me is preferred before me, whose shoe's latchet I am not not worthy to unloose." He was saying, "I'm not the Messiah, but He is the **coming one.**

Did you know that Job prophesied about Jesus? He said, "...I know that my redeemer liveth..." (Job 19:25). Job is a tremendous book, filled with vast knowledge, and is said to be one of the oldest books in the Bible. Historians say that Job was the first book ever written down—even before Moses wrote the Pentateuch!

How did Job have knowledge of a Redeemer if none of these prophesies were even recorded for him? I believe that God unfolded His story in the heavens. Job has more to say about the stars than any other book of the Bible! He probably received a wonderful revelation of the Lord from the very heavens themselves!

One of the principal or "decan" stars in Bootes is named **Arcturus,** and its name means "Watcher," or "Guardian." Job mentioned this star (Job 9:9, 38:32), and it further represents Jesus as the Guardian of His sheep: the Church. Notice that the sketch on page 20 shows Bootes with a shepherd's staff and sickle. Not only is Jesus the Good Shepherd, He is the "Lord of the great harvest" of souls!

> ". . . and then the sign of the Son of Man will appear in the sky, and then all the tribes of the earth will mourn, and they will see the Son of Man coming on the clouds of the sky with power and great glory" (Matthew 24:30 NAS).

> "And I looked, and behold a white cloud, and upon the cloud one sat like unto the Son of man, having on his head a golden crown, and in his hand a sharp sickle. . . . Thrust in thy sickle, and reap: for the time is come for thee to reap; for the harvest of the earth is ripe" (Revelation 14:14,15).

Only God Himself could bring these images together in such a beautiful manner! Now look at **Centaurus,** the fourth figure in the sign of Virgo. This figure is depicted as half-man and half-horse. It is symbolic of Jesus' nature, for He was both the Son of God, and the Son of man.

In His divine nature, Jesus was filled with the Spirit, filled with divine power in His earthly ministry: He worked miracles, raised the dead—and He was resurrected from the dead Himself! Yet in Jesus' physical body, He suffered as a human: He experienced thirst, pain, and the emotions of humanity. Until Jesus was born, no one had ever seen such a dual nature.

The Centaur depicts this contrasting nature, portraying both divinity and humanity. If you look at the figure you will see that he is carrying a long spear. I believe that it represents the sword of the Spirit (Ephesians 6:17), "which is the Word of God." In Revelation 19, Jesus returns in power and authority, wielding a sharp sword:

> "And I saw heaven opened, and behold a white horse; and he that sat upon him was called Faithful and True, and in righteousness he doth judge and make war. And he was clothed with a vesture dipped in blood; and his name is called the Word of God" (Revelation 19:11,13).

> "And out of his mouth goeth a sharp sword, that with it he should smite the nations: and he shall rule them with a rod of iron: and he treadeth the winepress of the fierceness and wrath of almighty God" (Revelation 19:15).

Just as in one life we are to conquer the works of darkness with the Word, Jesus will return to earth and forever cast the devil and his demons into the lake of fire.

Another decan star in the sign of Virgo, in the Centaur's figure is called "the despised." Jesus is the beloved Son of the Father, and He is our Lord—but the enemy really hates him, and influences others on earth who despised, hated and ultimately crucified Jesus. That's one thing about Jesus—no one can be "neutral" toward Him!

> "He is despised and rejected of men; a man of

sorrows, and acquainted with grief: and we hid as it were our faces from him; he was despised, and we esteemed him not" (Isaiah 53:3).

This Scripture shows a dramatic contrast to "the Desire of Nations"—and yet both figures are shown of one Man, Jesus, in the sign of Virgo! This seems to be a constellation which brings out the many-faceted personality of our Savior, and the many ways which people were affected by Him. His Own people despised and rejected Him, and yet to all others, and to some of His Own (the Jews), He was the Desired One. To the Gentiles He was the "Light" which was seen in great darkness.

The decan star called "the despised" is classified by scientists to be a "changeable star." It is constantly growing brighter every year. When I discovered this fact, I thought, "Isn't that just like the Lord! He is drawing our attention to a star which represents His growing influence in this world of darkness! There may be great darkness and sin in the world, but Jesus and His church are an even greater light!

The parallel shown here is that although opposition from Satan may grow stronger, Jesus in you will grow brighter as you shine the Gospel to the world. The next time that you're outside, point this star out to someone and tell them its significance; what a wonderful way to share Jesus!

The constellation of Virgo is a beautiful, intricate description of Jesus Christ—God and man. He was the virgin-born Child; the Seed of woman; the Branch of God; the Desire of all nations; the Son of God and Son of Man; and our great Shepherd and Harvester!

This exciting revelation of Jesus which is found in the Virgo constellation is only the ladder's first rung—you still have eleven more to climb! In the Bible, one very important character dreamed about a ladder which linked the earth to the heavens; his name was Jacob, the grandson of Abraham:

> "And he dreamed, and behold a ladder set up on the earth, and the top of it reached to heaven: and behold the angels of God were ascending and descending on it" (Genesis 28:12).

Through this dream, God directed Jacob's vision heavenward. He also wants you to focus your vision in the same direction! Can you see how the Zodiac, or "ladder," was meant to be a connection between heaven and earth? It was meant to reveal God's revelation knowledge to all men.

Only God could have conceived such a perfect, elaborate plan: one which shows His intentions for man from **before** the world's foundation. The Bible teaches that "Jesus is the Lamb slain from the foundation of the world" (Revelation 13:8), and you can know that God wrote His complete story in the stars before the world began. The next rung on the ladder is **Libra,** so prepare to discover what God has for you!

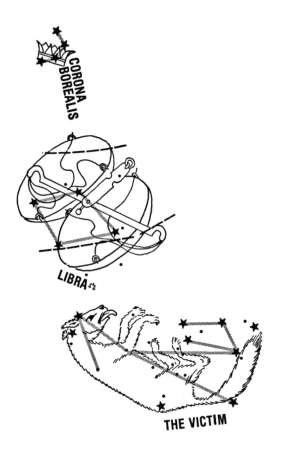

CORONA BOREALIS

LIBRA ♎

THE VICTIM

CRUX

CHAPTER TWO
LIBRA

"Who hath measured the waters in the hollow of his hand, and meted out heaven with the span, and comprehended the dust of the earth in a measure, and weighed the mountains in scales and the hills in a balance?" (Isaiah 40:12).

Isaiah speaks of the tremendous balance with which God created the universe. But in all the perfection of that balance, **Libra** presents scales which could never balance without Jesus having paid the price for our redemption. The Hebrew word for Libra is **Mozanaim,** which actually means "the scales weighing." Libra's scales describe God's eternal justice over the Church. There are four symbols in Libra; they are:

1. Libra: the scales;
2. Crux: the Southern Cross;
3. The Victim: a slain animal, and
4. Corona Borealis: a crown.

Daniel had some sobering things to say about man's side of the Libran scale:

"Thou art weighed in the balances, and found wanting" (Daniel 5:27). The side of the scales which is described here is pictured by a star called **Zuben al Genubi,** a meaning, "the price is deficient." If you and I had to make it to heaven on the merit of our own righteousness, it would not be enough; man's sinful nature is unacceptable to a holy God.

But if you accepted Jesus' sacrifice on Calvary, then you have received His righteousness as a gift. What will happen now, if you are "weighed in the balances?" Will you be found wanting? No! Now, with Jesus' perfect righteousness upon you, you will be found "complete in Him" (Col. 2:9).

Jesus' righteousness on your behalf is depicted in a star called **Zuben al Shemali,** which means "the price that covers." You could say that Jesus "jumped on the scales with us" and paid our debt to God. What a wonderful story of God's mercy toward us. The two stars, "the price is deficient" and "the price that covers," represent the old, old story of sinners who have received God's redeeming grace.

But if Jesus had not died on the cross for us, and taken our sin upon Himself, we could not be weighed on the scales and balance out! This aspect of God's plan for the Church is shown by the next symbol, the Southern Cross (Crux).

The cross in Libra is a sequence of stars with a fascinating history. It has been shifting southward in the heavens since Jesus' time—in fact, it was last seen on Jerusalem's horizon at about the time when Christ was crucified! Today, only certain areas of South America and Africa get occasional glimpses of the cross, which appears in the darkest part of the evening, just before dawn.

I think that the Southern Cross presents interesting symbology: When Jesus died on the cross, the sun was darkened, and there was no light in the sky. Now, those who have seen the Cross claim that its stars actually change in appearance, as daylight arrives—the cross seems to "bend" toward the earth. God still directs people to the saving power of Jesus through this cross in the stars!

Four very bright stars make up the cross's figure, and the

entire symbol is called **Adom,** meaning "to cut off." Daniel prophecied about its significance:

> "And after threescore and two weeks shall Messiah be cut off, but not for himself:..."
> (Daniel 9:26a).

Jesus "cut off" from His people, socially; Isaiah 53:3 reminds us that He would be **"despised** and **rejected** of men; a man of sorrows, and acquainted with grief." Verse eight continues the idea:

> "He was taken from prison and from judgment: and who shall declare his generation? for he was cut off out of the land of the living: for the transgression of my people was he stricken."

Jesus was truly "cut off" from His people, for they refused to recognize Him as the "desire of all nations," their Messiah. Instead, they made Him their Victim—which is the name of the next figure in the constellation of Libra. This represents Jesus, the slain Lamb of God Who took away the sins of the world. Without the shedding of His blood, there could have been no remission of our sin (Hebrews 9:22). Consider Galatians 3:13, which says that any man who "hangeth on a tree" is cursed. Jesus became the slain Lamb, upon Whom was the curse of all our sins.

The picture of the "victim" presents him as a strange looking animal; when I first saw the picture, I thought that he resembled a coyote, except that his ears were too pointed. Then after looking more closely at this picture, I found that this "victim" was actually a **lamb.** The ancients called him **Sura,** which means "sheep" or "lamb." Isaiah spoke of Jesus as the submissive lamb:

"...as a sheep before her shearers is dumb;
so he openeth not his mouth" (Isaiah 53:7b).

In the picture, the "victim" does look as though he's very quiet and submissive; also, notice that in this picture he is shown as having been slain by the Centaur's spear. He was slain by Himself? John 10:17-18 explains how:

"Therefore doth my Father love me, because I lay down my life, that I might take it again. **No man taketh it from me, but I lay it down of myself.** I have power to lay it down, and I have power to take it again...."

Jesus, because He was a willing sacrifice for the sins of the world, was, in effect, slain by His Own will. He Himself said, "No man can take my life." Because God was so merciful, and He foresaw man's fallen nature, He constructed this plan. He placed the victim, His cross, and the spear of deliverance as signs in the heavens; He gave us signs of the Lamb Who would be slain before the foundation of the world.

Throughout the Scriptures, beginning in Genesis with Cain and Abel, the slaying of a sacrificial lamb is shown. Abel was the first one to offer a slain lamb for a sacrifice unto the Lord:

"And Abel, he also brought of the firstlings of his flock and of the fat thereof. And the Lord had respect unto Abel and his offspring:..." (Genesis 4:4).

God loved and respected Abel's sacrifice because it was a **blood** sacrifice, one which is necessary for the remission of sin. Do you recall John the Baptist's words, when he saw Jesus? He revealed Jesus Christ as the "Victim:"

"The next day John seeth Jesus coming unto him, and saith, Behold the Lamb of God which taketh away the sin of the world" (John 1:29).

But because Jesus was the perfect sacrifice before God, He is now seated at the Father's right hand in the heavenlies, and He is wearing a crown of great honor. This is our last symbol in the sign of Libra, one which completes the perfect balance of the scales. Its name, **Corona Borealis** means, of course, "crown."

In this figure, notice that you can see the serpent, who represents Satan, heading in the crown's direction. He was not always a terrible serpent, though: at one time, he was the "anointed cherub" which covered God's throne. Ezekiel 28:14-17 describes what happened:

"Thou art the anointed cherub that covereth; and I have set thee so: thou wast upon the holy mountain of God; thou hast walked up and down in the midst of the stones of fire. Thou wast perfect in thy ways from the day that thou wast created till iniquity was found in thee. By the multitude of thy merchandise they have filled the midst of thee with violence, and thou hast sinned: therefore I will cast thee as profane out of the mountain of God: and I will destroy thee, O covering cherub, from the midst of the stones of fire. Thine heart was lifted up because of thy beauty, thou hast corrupted thy wisdom by reason of thy brightness: I will cast thee to the ground, I will lay thee before kings, that they may behold thee."

You can see that although Satan may have been cast out of heaven, he is still blinded by pride. That is why he's trying to get Jesus' crown. He knows that a part of his eternal punishment is that he will never attain a crown, while Jesus Christ is the One Who will receive many of them:

> "His eyes were as a flame of fire, and on his head were many crowns; and he had a name written, that no man knew, but he himself" (Revelation 19:12).

Hebrews 2:7,8 tells us that Jesus has a special crown from God, and I think that it's a tremendous description of His position as King of kings:

> "...thou crownedst him with glory and honor, and didst set him over the works of thy hands: Thou hast put all things in subjection under his feet...."

But the Scriptures have something even more exciting to say about Jesus' crown...and it is that He'll share it with us, His Body of believers:

> "And when the chief Shepherd shall appear, ye shall receive a crown of glory that fadeth not away" (I Peter 5:4).

> "...Who redeemeth thy life from destruction; who crowneth thee with loving-kindness and tender mercies;...(Psalm 103:4).

In Revelation 3:11, Jesus summoned Christians to hold fast to their faith until His return, and this is encouragement that He truly will "never leave nor forsake" us:

Behold, I come quickly: hold that fast which
thou hast, that no man take thy crown."

Libra is an exciting constellation. We may have been found
"wanting" on the scales of justice before we knew Jesus as
Savior; but He became our "price that covered," the "Victim"
Whose cross is the symbol of our salvation. Rejoice in the
crown of righteousness which He's given you, for the price is
no longer deficient—it's more than enough!

HERCULES

SERPENS

OPHIUCHUS

The Eoliptic or the Sun's Path

Antares

SCORPIO

CHAPTER THREE
SCORPIO

After Jesus' crucifixion, He descended into Hell, and when He left, with Him were the keys of Hell and death! He "...spoiled principalities and powers and rulers of darkness, making a great show of them openly..." (Colossians 2:15). Jesus' victory over Satan is the one that you'll see in the sign of **Scorpio;** four figures appear in this sign:

1. Scorpio: the scorpion, a symbol of Satan;
2. Ophiuchus: "the Serpent holder;"
3. Hercules: "the Strong Man;" and
4. Serpens: the snake.

The Hebrew root word for Scorpio means "a deadly foe," or "to cleave in conflict." Of course, the scorpion represents the foe whom Jesus defeated, Satan. In the star map, Hercules is shown with his foot upon Scorpio's head, and he's crushing it. His right heel is drawn back, as though it has been stung by the scorpion's tail, which is where the scorpion holds the semi-paralyzing poison. Intense pain is the result of a scorpion's bite, and here you can see a representation of the painful sting of sin. Once again, we see reference to the key Scripture already mentioned in the first chapter:

> And I will put enmity between thee and the woman, and between thy seed and her seed; it

shall bruise thy head, and thou shalt bruise
his heel" (Genesis 3:15).

Satan knew that God would send the "Seed of woman" to
"bruise his head" and defeat him. In the sign of Scorpio, a
man is bruising the scorpion's head, while at the same time,
the scorpion is bruising the man's heel. The devil is so
blind—he never realized that crucifying Jesus would bring
about his own destruction:

> "Which none of the princes of this world
> knew: for had they known it, they would not
> have crucified the Lord of glory" (I Corin-
> thians 2:8).

Ophiuchus is the name of the man in this sequence of
stars, and he is a "figure" of Jesus. Here is the symbology:
When Jesus was crucified, He endured Satan's sting of death
by taking all the poison of our sin upon Himself. Jesus took
our place and received upon Himself the sting which should
have been upon us; He delivered us from sin's poison. The
apostle Paul boasted of Jesus' triumph:

> "...Death is swallowed up in victory. O
> death, where is thy sting? O grave where is thy
> victory? The sting of death is sin; and the
> strength of sin is the law. But thanks be to
> God, which giveth us the victory through our
> Lord Jesus Christ" (I Corinthians 15:54b-57).

But in order to obtain that victory for us, Jesus had to
undergo affliction; this affliction is shown in the principal star
of Scorpio, called **Antares,** which means "wounding," "cutting" or "tearing." The prophet Isaiah wrote about this great
affliction which was upon the Lord:

40

> "Surely he hath born our griefs and carried our sorrows: yet we did esteem him stricken, smitten with God, and afflicted. But he was wounded for our transgressions, he was bruised for our iniquities: the chastisement of our peace was upon him; and with his stripes we are healed" (Isaiah 53:4,5).

Jesus' back was cut with cruel scourging; His flesh was torn as Roman soldiers pounded stakes through His hands and feet, into the wood of the cross. He endured the "bruising of His heel" for one reason: to destroy the scorpion's paralyzing sting so that you could be free of death.

The freedom which Jesus has obtained for you can also be seen in the next segment of stars, which shows a man restraining a huge serpent in his hands. The Scriptures speak of Satan as being a serpent again and again; even his original "picture" in the garden of Eden shows Satan as a serpent. This constellation shows the serpent attempting to steal the man's crown; but the man, whose name is **Ophiuchus,** has dominion, and his control over the serpent is obvious.

Who is Ophiuchus? He is "the chief who cometh," representing our soon-coming King, Jesus Christ. This constellation illustrates Jesus' total control over Satan, and shows you how He obtained that control: through the bruising of His heel. That should really make us feel secure! You don't ever have to fear death, because Jesus is in control:

> "Forasmuch then as the children are partakers of flesh and blood, he also himself likewise took part of the same; that through death he might destroy him that had the power of death, that is, the devil; And deliver them who through fear of death were all their lifetime subject to bondage" (Hebrews 2:14,15).

41

So far, you have seen symbols which have represented Jesus Christ in many Scriptural ways: the Branch, the Seed, the Chief Who cometh, etc. But the sign of Scorpio is rich with symbology, and I think you'll really like this next portrayal of Jesus. He is shown on the star map as a man called **Hercules,** and his strength is very evident in this picture—his foot is firmly planted on the head of a dragon, called **Draco.** (A dragon is another Biblical symbol for Satan). The psalmist did an excellent job of describing this set of stars:

> "...the dragon shalt thou trample under feet" (Psalm 91:13).

Hercules is a figure which represents power, just as all power belongs to Jesus Christ:

> "And Jesus came and spake unto them, saying, All power is given unto me in heaven and in earth" (Matthew 28:18).

On Hercules' head is a bright star which is also symbolic of Jesus' might; the star is called **Ras al Gethi,** meaning, "the head of him who bruises." Again, you can see a representation of Jesus defeating the dragon, Satan. But there is a star in the knee of Hercules which balances the great power of Jesus—it represents His submission to God's perfect will.

The star which is shown in Hercules' knee is translated to mean "the branch kneeling." This again brings in a facet of the Virgo constellation, which describes Jesus as "the Branch," in agreement with prophecy.

I believe that the contrast of might (Hercules) and submission to God (kneeling) which is shown in this constellation is something that all Christians should remember: It is true that, in Christ, we share the same dominion that He has. But we are also to remember that we are His **servants.** Jesus

Himself said, ". . . the Son of man came not to be ministered unto, but to minister, and to give his life a ransom for many" (Mark 10:45).

I wondered about a specific time when the Branch, Jesus Christ, physically knelt in submission to God. The Lord showed me where He did kneel. He knelt before God in the garden of Gethsemne, only moments before His Own disciple, Judas, betrayed Him. These are the words that he spoke:

> ". . . O my Father, if it be possible, let this cup
> pass from me: nevertheless not as I will, but as
> thou wilt" (Matthew 26:39).

The Messiah, Lord of all might and power, did not have to kneel. He did not have to take our affliction upon Himself, but He chose to lay His might aside and become our Savior. There aren't many fair deals in the world today, but Jesus gave us a deal that is more than fair; His mercy is shown in every one of the constellations you've seen. Virgo shows Him as the Shepherd Who will return to claim us as His Own; Libra shows that the scales could not balance out—until Jesus was balancing His righteousness with ours; now you have seen that He destroyed the poison of sin and death, and gave us His life. It's no wonder that David said, "The heavens declare the glory of God; . . ." (Psalm 19:1).

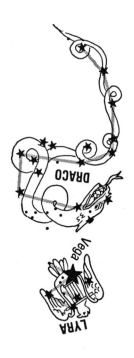

DRACO

Vega

LYRA

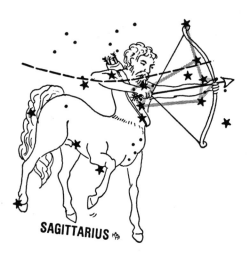

SAGITTARIUS

ARA

CHAPTER FOUR
SAGITTARIUS

Draco, the dragon from the constellation of Scorpio, is a carryover into this sign—and he's about to be shot by an archer named **Sagittarius.** There are four major figures in this sign:

1. Sagittarius: the Archer;
2. Lyra: the harp;
3. Ara: a funeral pyre; and
4. Draco: the dragon.

Just as the dragon is seen in Sagittarius, as well as in Scorpio, you will also discover a similarity in the Sagittarian archer to the centaur in Virgo. The archer is shown as being "half-man and half-horse," another portrayal of Jesus' dual nature, mingling divinity and humanity into one. In this figure, you will see Him as both the Son of man and the Son of God.

The Revelation of John speaks of Jesus as the archer, who sends forth arrows of truth and judgment! A feeling of swiftness is this sign's nature; I get the impression that something is going to happen very, very quickly:

> "Behold I come quickly: blessed is he that keepeth the sayings of the prophecy of this book" (Revelation 22:7).

> "And behold, I come quickly; and my reward
> is with me, . . ." (Revelation 22:12).

These Scriptures speak of the speed with which Jesus will return; I Thessalonians tells about how His return will affect those who aren't watching:

> "For when they shall say, Peace and safety;
> then sudden destruction cometh upon
> them, . . ." (I Thessalonians 5:3).

God's righteous arrows of truth and judgment will shock a lot of people who were scoffers, rather than **watchers.** Paul prophesied about this in II Timothy 3:1-2.

> "This know also, that in the last days perilous
> times shall come. For men shall be lovers of
> their own selves, covetous, boasters, proud,
> blasphemers, disobedient to parents, un-
> thankful, unholy, . . ."

What is going to happen in the "perilous times" of such disobedience? Jesus will return for us like a "thief in the night." But until He returns, we are supposed to "occupy," and be witnesses of Him wherever we go. Sagittarius carries the idea that Jesus gave us His Own power and ability to be His witnesses.

While the principal star in Scorpio meant "wounding," "cutting," or "tearing," in the Sagittarian constellation, you see the archer sending out a deadly arrow into His opponent's heart. We may be in a costly war, but we know that we **win** in the end!

Now focus your attention directly above the warrior and you will see a harp. **Lyra** is representative of the rejoicing of the saints who overcome in Christ. The history of the lyre can be traced back to the book of Genesis:

> "And his brother's name was Jubal: he was
> the father of all such as handle the harp and
> organ" (Genesis 4:21).

One star in this harp shines very brightly, called **Vega,** and this word is full of meaning: "He shall be exalted, the warrior triumphant." If we consider the lyre to be an instrument of praise, then the exaltation of Jesus, our Warrior, is certainly something to praise Him about!

I've found that the harp always symbolizes praise and worship—and its significance is growing, for if ever we lived in a time of praise and worship, it's today! It seems that wherever you go, people are involved in worshiping the Lord. And what happened in the Bible when people praised Him? God came right into their situations! Psalm 22:3 agrees, saying, "God inhabits the praise of (His people) Israel," and **you** are spiritual Israel; you are the seed of Abraham by faith. If you want God to put you over in any situation, take the psalmist's advice—praise Him! You say, "Is it that important?" It's that important: I believe that praise and worship will unite the Body of Christ, and cause Him to return in the clouds, to catch His Church unto Himself; in the twinkling of an eye, we'll be with Jesus forever. Be a part of His welcoming committee: start praising Him! Finally, notice that the lyre is being held by an eagle: the eagle is symbolic of overcoming, symbolizing that Jesus returns to us as the King Who rises above all.

Not every figure in the Sagittarian constellation looks as positive as those of Hercules, or Lyre. The next series of stars forms a funeral pyre called **Ara,** When I first saw it, I thought it really looked negative. Then, something else caught my eye: this pyre is very unusual, because it is upside-down, and the fire is coming from underneath it! I realized why the flames are blazing downward: to signify that Satan will be cast **down** into the Lake of Fire, where he will burn forever. Ara is a sign of the devil's own funeral pyre.

Have you found him in the picture? He is the horrible looking dragon, just beyond the figure of the eagle which holds the lyre. This figure is shown in an attempt to exalt himself—it's no surprise, because he was thrown out of heaven itself for the same sin: exalting himself in pride.

Another interesting point about Draco is that he is the most noticeable constellation which you can see in the heavens, because of his conspicuous size. But in the constellation of Sagittarius, you can see that his size doesn't really matter—the archer is aiming his arrow to kill Draco anyway; and his funeral prye has been prepared. In the end, all nations will look upon Satan, wondering how he could ever have distorted God's truth. The Bible says that people will say, "This is the one who deceived nations? Why did he think that he was such a big deal?"

Draco represents Satan, and I think that God had that star named especially to remind Satan of his future. The dragon's name has a very just meaning: "the trodden on." His chief star is called **Al Waid,** which means "he who is to be destroyed." Isn't that descriptive! It's no surprise that Satan didn't want us to see what is really proclaimed in the stars—his fall, and future destruction is advertised in them, from one end of the heavens to the other!

God did more than just tell us that Satan's power has been spoiled, though. He wants us to know that Satan doesn't try to harm people through any different tricks than the ones he used on Eve—deception. That's why the star called **Thuban** gains so much in translation, for it means "the head of the subtle." He may be sly, but he's also defeated. Some of the other stars in this constellation finish the description: 1) **Grumain,** "the deceiver;" 2) **El A Thik,** "the fraudful;" 3) **El A sieh,** "the humbled;" and 4) **Gianser,** "a punished enemy."

By the time that I discovered all of these names, be sure that there was no doubt in my mind that these stars were divinely named. God has always known that Satan was a liar, and that he would be destroyed; these names are His way of letting us know the sureness of His plan.

What will happen to the serpent, Draco? He loses. Hell was prepared for Satan and his archangels. God's Word says that they will burn in the Lake of Fire forever, when judgment day arrives:

> "In that day the Lord his sore and great and strong sword shall punish leviathan the piercing serpent, even leviathan that crooked serpent; and he shall slay the dragon that is in the sea" (Isaiah 27:1).

If God saw ahead to place signs of His plan in the heavens—then don't you think that He saw ahead for your provision in a trial? God made a plan in the very beginning to deliver you from the "piercing serpent," Satan. So if you're in a trial today, look to God's provision for your deliverance: His Son, Jesus Christ!

When Jesus lived here as a man, almost two-thousand years ago, He became flesh like you and me so that He could remove our sin. These first four signs have dealt specifically with Jesus' life and death, showing just **how** He defeated Satan to set **you** free! The next four signs are directly related to the lives of every born-again believer, because they show the work of Jesus Christ with the church.

Now see how you can **stand as a conqueror** in the victory that He's won!

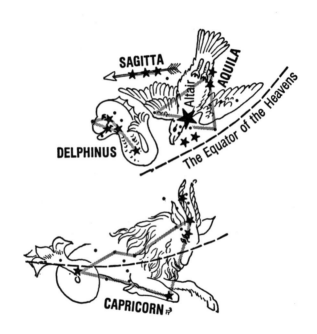

CHAPTER FIVE
CAPRICORN

The first four signs that you studied show the person of Jesus, His work and His triumph over the enemy, Satan. The next four signs, beginning with the constellation of **Capricornus,** relate to the fruits of Jesus' finished work and His position as our mediator. These signs will show the church and the many benefits we can claim because we have been redeemed by the sacrifice of our Savior, Jesus. The following symbols are associated with the sign of Capricorn:

1. Capricorn; the goat;
2. Sagitta: the arrow;
3. Aquila: the dying eagle; and
4. Delphinus: the dolphin.

The goat, Capricorn, appears to be dying, and is always pictured with one of his legs tucked under his body, while the other leg appears to be weak. In the Old Testament, goats were often used for the sacrifice:

> "And Moses diligently sought the goat of the sin offering. . ." (Leviticus 10:16).

> "Take ye a kid of the goats for a sin offering. . ." (Leviticus 9:3).

Capricorn is symbolic of Jesus, our sacrifice of atonement,

Who was "wounded for our transgressions and bruised for our iniquities" (Isaiah 53:5). You say, "I thought that Jesus was our sacrificial Lamb; He wasn't a goat." But he was! He was our **scapegoat.** You have probably seen someone in your home or office take the blame for another's mistake at one time or another; Jesus was the One Who took the blame for our sin. But did you know the term "scapegoat" originated in the Old Testament?

One goat of atonement was killed in the place of sinful people, as a sacrifice for their sin; he was the "sin offering." But in order to choose a goat for the sin offering, two goats would be brought in and lots would be cast to determine which would be offered. The goat which was not offered became the Israelites' "scapegoat." He would "carry their sins" into the wilderness, away from the camp, never to be seen again. Leviticus 16:7-10 describes God's commands concerning the scapegoat and the goat of atonement:

> "And he shall take the two goats, and present them before the Lord at the door of the tabernacle of the congregation. And Aaron shall cast lots upon the two goats; one lot for the Lord, and the other lot for the scapegoat. And Aaron shall bring the goat upon which the Lord's lot fell, and offer him for a sin offering. But the goat, on which the lot fell to be the scapegoat, shall be presented alive before the Lord, to make an atonement with him, and to let him go for a scapegoat into the wilderness."

It is true that Jesus was our Lamb, slain before the foundation of the world; but to understand the full picture of salvation, you must also see Him as your scapegoat. The name **Capricornus** beautifully completes this idea, because it really means "atonement."

Remember, your sins were not only forgiven—they were also carried away and forgotten. I'm sure that Satan doesn't want the word "atonement" written across the skies, but God's story is there, intended to direct men toward their Savior.

Has the goat, our symbol of atonement, been counterfeited? Yes! It has been used as a symbol in satanic worship. But keep in mind that Satan never creates—he only deceives and tries to falsify the truth which God has created. You are not to reject the symbol of the goat but the lies that the devil has told about that symbol. He just didn't want people to know that Jesus became our goat of atonement so that He could make us His spotless lambs!

Capricorn's chief stars are **Gedi** and **Dabih,** meaning "the cut off" and "the sacrifice slain." And the goat has another very peculiar characteristic—he has the tail of a fish! In the picture, the impression is that the fish is being born of the goat; it displays the **new birth** of the Church as the final outcome of the suffering in atonement. If Jesus had not died and been your scapegoat, then you could not have put your old nature to death and experienced new life in Him! Christ spoke of this new birth in John 3:5:

> "Jesus answered, Verily, verily, I say unto thee, Except a man be born of water and of the Spirit, he cannot enter into the kingdom of God."

The symbol of the fish relates to born-again Christians. The Green initials of "Jesus Christ, Son of God, Savior" form the word **ichtus,** which means "fish." In the early years after Jesus' crucifixion and resurrection, believers would meet secretly, due to heavy persecution on Christians, and they would scratch the symbol of a fish on the ground with a stick—this was their way of greeting one another in the name of the Lord Jesus Christ. The constellation of Capricorn gives you a vivid picture of the new birth of the Church: it shows Christ's body of believers emerging through the process of His crucifixion, death, and subsequent resurrection.

The next figure in the sign of Capricorn is an arrow called **Sagitta,** which has been shot from Sagittarius' bow. Heading straight for its target, an eagle called Aquila, whose arrow is this? It is the arrow of the Lord as seen in II Kings 13:14-17:

> "Now Elisha was fallen sick of his sickness whereof he died. And Joash the king of Israel came down unto him, and wept over his face, and said, O my father, my father, the chariot of Israel, and the horseman thereof. And Elisha said unto him, take bow and arrows. And he took unto him bow and arrows. And he said to the king of Israel, Put thine hand upon the bow. And he put his hand upon it: and Elisha put his hands upon the king's hands. And he said, Open the window eastward. And he opened it. Then Elisha said, Shoot. And he shot. And he said, **The arrow of the Lord's deliverance,** and the arrow of deliverance from Syria: for thou shalt smite the Syrians in Aphek, till thou have consumed them."

What was the arrow of the Lord's deliverance? It was, and still is, the Word of God! His arrow cannot be bound once it has been sent out to accomplish God's works. God's Word is His arrow, and it will bring you deliverance from your enemies just as it was Israel's deliverance from Syria in the passage from II Kings. Ephesians 6:12 tells you who you will slay when you speak the Word:

> "For we wrestle not against flesh and blood, but against principalities, against powers, against the rulers of the darkness of this world, against spiritual wickedness in high places."

God has a strategy for you that no enemy can gainsay nor resist! He has said, "So shall my word be that goeth forth out of thy mouth: it shall not return unto me void, but it shall accomplish that which I please, and it shall prosper in the thing whereto I sent it" (Isaiah 55:11). You can send the arrow of God's deliverance to accomplish miracles in any situation! Be assured that when you do, by speaking God's Word to your circumstances, you'll see results!

The next symbol in the sign of Capricorn is a falling eagle, called **Aquila.** Its principal star is named **Al Tair,** meaning ing "the wounded one." The secondary star means "the scarlet covered one," and the next star is translated to mean "the torn one." Finally, the fourth star in Aquila completes the description for it means "the one who was wounded in the heel." Obviously, this segment of stars is meant to describe Jesus Christ and His suffering on Mount Calvary: He was wounded for our sins; He was covered in scarlet through the scourging of men and hanging upon the cross; His flesh was torn and beaten; and He was "wounded in the heel" to fulfill the prophecy in Genesis 3:15.

The names of the stars in Aquila may not seem to present a very victorious scene, but let me assure you that further typology creates a much more positive picture. This eagle has been shot by an arrow (the Living Word of God), so again there is the comparison that says, "Jesus' suffering may have occurred at the hands of men—but it was by the will of God." Isaiah 53:10 finishes the idea:

"Yet **it pleased the Lord to bruise him;** he hath put him to grief: when thou shalt make his soul an offering for sin, he shall see his seed, he shall prolong his days, and the pleasure of the Lord shall prosper in his hand."

It was Jesus' tremendous love for you and me that gave Him the ability to undergo the "bruising" of taking our sin upon Himself; He knew that afterwards, He would "see His seed." Who is His seed? That is you and I and every born-again Christian who has become the "seed of Abraham" by faith:

"Therefore it is of faith, that it might be by grace; to the end the promise might be sure to all the seed; not to that only which is of the law, but to that also which is of the faith of Abraham; who is the father of us all" (Romans 4:16).

I have always found the study of eagles to be interesting: they build huge nests with twigs and straws, and the mother eagle even uses fine feathers, plucked from her own breast. Her little eaglets must have a happy time in the nest because it is just as warm and soft as it can be. Eagles are also known for the fact that their youth is renewed in the latter part of their lives. As their sight grows dim and their bodies begin to grow old, they separate themselves from the other birds. Alone, the eagle will pluck out all of its feathers and beat his beak against a rocky wall until it comes off. Forced to fast, this must be a time when the eagle appears that he cannot possibly live; but as his beak grows back in, and his feathers grow back in, what happens? He is renewed, to live twice as long; **his lifespan doubles!**

In the constellation of Capricorn, the eagle is symbolic of

Jesus, Who, by taking our death upon Himself, destroyed death and had his youth returned through resurrection! But Jesus did far more than double His lifespan—His life is now eternal, and He offers that complete renewal to all those who are in Him. Resurrection life and power can strengthen every area of your life, for in Jesus Christ there is no darkness—only light and life. Now we can sit with Christ in heavenly places because we are His Body.

The Lord ministered in a very special way to Jacob. The Scripture compares His tenderness to an eagle. It reminds me of what the Bible calls "meekness," for it is a special combination of strength and gentleness. If you're in a situation that seems like a "wilderness," let this Scripture speak to you.

> "He [God] found him in a desert land, and in the waste howling wilderness; he led him about, he instructed him, he kept him as the apple of his eye. As an eagle stirreth up her nest, fluttereth over her young, spreadeth abroad her wings, taketh them, beareth them on her wings: So the Lord alone did lead him, and there was no strange god with him. He made him ride on the high places of the earth, that he might eat the increase of the fields. ." (Deuteronomy 32:10-13).

Remember, it's always easier to "ride upon the Father's wings" than try to get somewhere with your own. Have you ever tried to "flap your own wings?" You didn't get very far, did you? Allow God to minister to you with His special quality of strength and gentleness; He wants you to soar above any wilderness in your life by receiving your peace from Him.

Now receive a view of the "mature" Church in the next constellation which is called **Delphinus,** the dolphin. You saw the "fish-goat" symbol which showed the new birth emerging from Christ's atonement. Now, Delphinus is depicted as a grown fish leaping with great energy. I see this as the mature Church of Jesus Christ which is utilizing and experiencing the fullness of life in Him.

Perhaps Revelation 1:5,6 offers the most complete view of the dolphin's image:

> "And from Jesus Christ, who is the faithful witness, and the first begotten of the dead, and the prince of the kings of the earth. Unto him **that loved us,** and **washed us from our sins in his own blood,** and **hath made us kings and priests unto God** and his Father; to him be glory and dominion for ever and ever. Amen."

Like this dolphin, it is Jesus' desire for us to rise up from the water of new birth, and show His energy to the world to give them hope. In September, at midnight, the sign of Delphinus, the dolphin, is displayed in the heavens for all to see—our blessed hope of attaining the fullness of the measure of our stature in Jesus Christ.

Look at the order of the stars in this constellation: first, you saw the arrow of God's deliverance, His Word, piercing His Son, Jesus Christ—because we are His Body, the arrow pierces us, too. Then, you see the resurrective power of God's Word causing Jesus to be renewed, as He rose into His permanent glory at the right hand of God. Finally, because of the piercing of God's Word and the renewal of Jesus' life, you see Delphinus representing the Church in its full maturity.

In the sign of Capricorn, the "new birth" of a vital, energetic Church emerged from Jesus' offering Himself as our atonement. But the exciting part is, Jesus did more than renew us—He gave us His Holy Spirit so that we could **stay**

renewed. In the next sign, Aquarius, you see that God had the outpouring of His Spirit in mind from the earth's beginning!

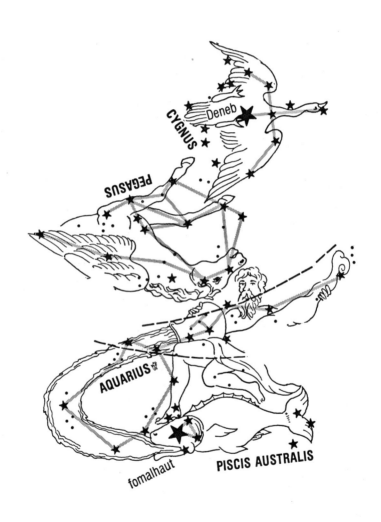

CYGNUS

Deneb

PEGASUS

AQUARIUS

PISCIS AUSTRALIS

fomalhaut

CHAPTER SIX
AQUARIUS

After Jesus Christ died and became the atonement for our sin, He was resurrected into new and eternal life with the Father. Now, in Him, we share in His abundant life on earth and will have eternal life with Him. The apostles desired Jesus to continue in earthly ministry, but He told them. "...it is expedient for you that I go away: for if I go not away, the Comforter will not come unto you; but if I depart, I will send him unto you" (John 16:7). The word Aquarius means "outpouring," and symbolizes the fulfillment of this prophecy: the outpouring of the Holy Spirit to bring new life and power into the Church. Aquarius has four symbols:

1. Aquarius: the Waterman;
2. Piscis Australis: the Southern Fish;
3. Pegasus: the Winged Horse; and
4. Cygnus: the Swan.

In the illustration on the star map, Aquarius is shown seated, and he holds a large vase, or vessel in his hand. Water is being poured out of the vessel in abundance, and it is flowing from the east to the west. Compare this to the Gospel's outpouring, which began in the east and flowed into the western world.

There is something else which is unusual about this picture—it is that the water increases in volume as it flows downward. It is purposely being poured into the mouth of a large fish, which is shown drinking from the unending stream. The fish is symbolic of the Body of Christ, drinking of "living water" as prophesied by Jesus in John 4:13,14, as He spoke to a Samaritan woman:

> "Whosoever drinketh of this water shall thirst again: But whosoever drinketh of the water that I shall give him shall never thirst; but the water that I shall give him shall be in him a well of water springing up into everlasting life."

What is this water that Jesus talked about? It is the baptism in the Holy Spirit, with which we can all be **filled!**

Today, increasing numbers of people are welcoming and receiving the baptism in the Holy Spirit in their lives. Joel prophesied that they would, and you and I have the privilege of living in the day when his prophecy is being fulfilled. Everywhere, people are proclaiming that an immersion in God's Living Water will transform lives forever:

> "And it shall come to pass afterward, that I will pour out my spirit upon all flesh; and your sons and daughters shall prophesy, your old men shall dream dreams, your young men shall see visions: And also upon the servants and upon the handmaids in those days will I pour out my spirit" (Joel 2:28,29).

The name of the principal star in this sign of Aquarius is **Sa'ad a Melik** and it means "the record of the outpouring." The record of the outpouring of the Holy Spirit is, of course, God's Word. Jesus Himself bare record in John 7:38:

"He that believeth on me, as the scripture hath said, out of his belly shall flow rivers of living water."

The baptism in the Holy Spirit wasn't something that God just "came up with" in New Testament times—the prophet Isaiah said, "the glorious Lord will be unto us a place of broad rivers and streams" (Isaiah 33:21).

Do you remember the account of Exodus 15, when Moses left Egypt with the children of Israel? He led them from the Red Sea out into the "wilderness of Shur." By then, after three days in the wilderness, the children of Israel ran into a real problem: they found themselves without water! The Hebrew people which Moses had led out of bondage, were very angry and worried, so they started murmuring against him.

Finally, they discovered a place called **Marah,** which means "bitter," where there was water to quench their thirst. You can imagine their distress when they tasted the water and discovered that it was far too bitter to drink!

"And when they came to Marah, they could not drink of the waters of Marah, for they were bitter; therefore the place of it was called Marah. And the people murmured against Moses, saying, What shall we drink? And he cried unto the Lord; and the Lord shewed him a tree, which when he had cast into the waters, the waters were made sweet: there he made for them a statute and an ordinance, and there he proved them" (Exodus 15:23-25).

After the miracle in the wilderness, the children of Israel again experienced great thirst after reaching camp at a place called Rephidim. Here, they saw God manifest His miracle power again! God told Moses to pick up the staff with which he had worked many supernatural signs—and He said, "Hit the rock with your staff, Moses!" When he hit the rock of Horeb, the Israelites' trial of thirst was solved again:

> ". . . and you shall strike the rock, and water
> will come out of it, that the people may drink"
> (Exodus 17:6 NAS).

Who did that rock represent? It symbolized Jesus, our "Rock of ages." This event foreshadowed our Redeemer and source of Living Water—and He should be our only source of water for every day of our lives! The apostle Paul spoke to the Corinthians about Jesus as their Rock and source of water:

> "Moreover, brethren, I would not that ye
> should be ignorant, how that all our fathers
> were under the cloud, and all passed through
> the sea; And were all baptized unto Moses in
> the cloud and in the sea; And did all eat the
> same spiritual meat; And did all drink the
> same spiritual drink: for they drank of that
> spiritual Rock that followed them: and that
> Rock was Christ" (I Corinthians 10:1-4).

The people of Israel didn't see the water until Moses struck the rock—but it was still there all the time! Isn't that just like Jesus: anyone who calls upon Him will find Him.

But the Bible is so practical; God did more than just tell us that He would be our source of Living Water; He also provided us with a way to **receive it** as reality in our lives! Numbers 21:16,17 is an exciting story which is a fine example of how you can ask for the water of the Holy Spirit:

"And from thence they went to Beer: that is
the well whereof the Lord spake unto Moses,
Gather the people together, and I will give
them water. Then Israel sang this song,
Spring up, O well; sing ye unto it."

As the Israelites began singing, "Spring up, O well," the
waters began bubbling up to the well's surface!

It is the same principle with being baptized in the Holy
Spirit: you don't have to beg, because the water is already
there. You just have to ask, according to Luke 11:13, which
says, "If you then being evil, know how to give good gifts unto
your children: how much more shall your heavenly Father
give the Holy Spirit to them that ask him?" All that you must
do to receive God's outpouring is to ask! It's that simple.

Sometimes even after you receive the Holy Spirit, you may
feel as though your "well" is running dry; you may want a
fresh zeal in your walk with the Lord. When this happens,
sing praises to the Lord, as the children of Israel did! Dig into
the Word of God, just as they dug the well—you may not see
the water (they didn't either!), but start "digging" by faith
because Jesus' water of life is within you ready to spring up in
your heart!

Look at **Piscis Australis,** the "Southern Fish" on your
star map. He is shown drinking from the river, which is held
by the mighty Aquarian man. The world today is full of "thirs-
ty fish." You were once one! But as you were filled with Jesus'
Holy Spirit, wonderful renewal became yours. Now you may
pray and even sing in the Spirit; you make positive confes-
sions of your faith by speaking God's Word to your situation
realizing that "life and death are in the power of the tongue"
(Proverbs 18:21). Why? Because you received "power from
on high" which enables you to walk in the fullness of the
glory that Christ has for His Church. Before Jesus' death and
resurrection, He said that **believers** were supposed to receive

the Holy Spirit:

> "In the last day, that great day of the feast, Jesus stood and cried, saying, If any man thirst let him come unto me, and drink. He that believeth on me, as the scripture hath said, out of his belly shall flow rivers of living water. (But this spake he of the Spirit, which they that believe on him should receive..." (John 7:37-39).

Then, after Jesus' ascension to the Father, one of the last utterances which He personally spoke to the disciples was regarding the Holy Spirit, and the power which would enter their lives:

> "But ye shall receive power, after that the Holy Ghost is come upon you: and ye shall be witnesses unto me both in Jerusalem, and in all Judea, and in Samaria, and unto the uttermost part of the earth" (Acts 1:8).

It is important that believers realize that Jesus gave us the outpouring of His Spirit for more than just "having power." He gave us that power to be His witnesses! It's an exciting thought to know that today we possess the same Holy Spirit within us which was within Jesus so that we can be witnesses who are able to share His Living Water wherever we go!

As we begin sharing Jesus' Living Water from our "earthen vessels," we can be sure that His return is not far off. That's what the constellation of **Pegasus** is all about. Flying forward with great speed, as shown on the star map, this winged horse's name means "the chief that is returning." When you see the outpouring of Jesus' Spirit upon all flesh, be sure that Jesus is returning soon to gather His Church unto Himself!

How fast will Jesus come to earth to remove His Church from this world? I Corinthians 15:52 tells us that this will happen "In a moment, in the twinkling of an eye!"

The ancient titles of the stars in the constellation of Pegasus describe our returning Lord: **Markab,** "the returning;" **Scheat,** "he who goeth and returneth;" **Enif,** "the branch;" **Al Genib,** "who carries;" **Homan,** "the waters;" **Matar,** "who causeth the plenteous overflow." The names of these stars paint a "picture" of Jesus' return with a clarity that could only be supernatural!

The books of Isaiah and Revelation both show Jesus as returning to earth for judgment, riding upon a horse. (We studied this in the chapter on Virgo.) Truly, Christ **is** the Returning One, Who is coming again with power and might. Just the thought of His return should quicken our hearts and bring us great joy:

> "For the Lord himself shall descend from heaven with a shout, with the voice of the archangel, and with the trump of God: and the dead in Christ shall rise first: Then we which are alive and remain shall be caught up together with them in the clouds, to meet the Lord in the air: and so shall we ever be with the Lord. **Wherefore comfort one another with these words"** (I Thessalonians 4:16-18).

Then, Revelation 22:1 and 17 offer insight on what the outpouring of Living Water will be like, and what we can expect before Jesus' return:

> "And he shewed me a pure river of water of life, clear as crystal, proceeding out of the throne of God and of the Lamb."

"And the Spirit and the bride say, Come. And
let them that heareth say, Come. And let him
that is athirst come. And whosoever will, let
him take the water of life freely."

The sign of Jesus' return is found in this constellation, and
it is tied in with the outpouring of the Holy Spirit. For centuries, men have known that the great outpouring signals His
second coming. Judging from the signs that we have seen in
our century, we should be "looking up" knowing that our
redemption is drawing near!

The last accompanying figure in the sign of Aquarius is a
swan, whose name is **Cygnus.** Eighty-one stars make up this
constellation, and they confirm the sureness of Jesus' great
harvest of His Church, the "Rapture" or "Catching Away."
Four of the brightest stars make up the shape of a cross; the
clearest of the four stars is called **Deneb,** meaning "the Lord
or Judge to come." The other three are: **Azel,** "who goes and
returns;" **Fafage,** "glorious, shining forth;" and **Sadr,** "who
returns as in a circle." These are only a sampling of the stars
which compose the constellation of the swan, Cygnus. Two
more of them confirm the theme: **Adige,** which means "flying
swiftly," and **Arided** "he shall come down."

I was amazed at how these symbols and names of the stars
correspond with the written Word of God! It is no
coincidence; it was God's purpose from creation's beginning!

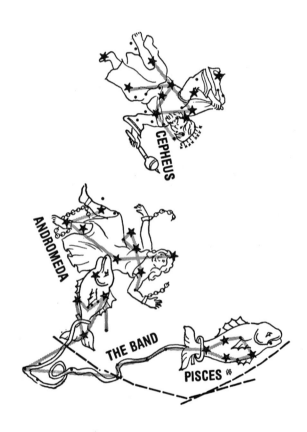

CEPHEUS

ANDROMEDA

THE BAND

PISCES ♓

CHAPTER SEVEN
PISCES

Pisces, which means "fish," expands on the theme of the church which was seen in the signs of Capricornus, Sagittarius and Aquarius. This exciting sign describes and further symbolizes the fullness of the Church after the resurrection of Jesus Christ. Several symbols appear:

1. Pisces: the two Fish;
2. Cepheus: the King;
3. Andromeda: the Woman; and
4. The Band.

Not one fish, but two are shown in the constellation of Pisces, with one swimming in the direction of the North Pole, and the other swimming toward the sun. Although both fish are shown as swimming in separate directions, they are tied together by a cord which is called "Al Risha." The single cord provides a "common" bond between the two fish, and is held in the forearm of a lamb who will be featured in the next sign of the Zodiac, Aries. The two fish appear to be under the control of the lamb.

Are there two Churches? No, but these fish represent an Old Covenant, and a New Covenant which gives us new and better promises to fulfill God's Covenant under the Abrahamic Law: they are the Old and New Testament Churches!

Even though they are swimming in different directions, they are held in the forearm of Jesus, the Lamb, and the cord definitely points to the fact that the old is tied to the new. Matthew 13:52 explains why both the Old and New Testament Churches are important:

> "...Therefore every scribe which is instructed unto the kingdom of heaven is like unto a man that is an householder, which bringeth forth out of his treasure things **new and old.**"

The two Churches are companions: the Old Covenant was the basis on which God created his New Covenant. Without each other, they are incomplete, for the New Covenant cannot stand alone, but rather must fulfill the Old one!

Just as the Church of the Old Testament focused on the sacrificial lamb, the Church of the New Testament focuses upon the ultimate Sacrifice, the Lamb of God, Jesus Christ! Hebrews 11:40 says, "God having provided some better thing for us, that they without us should not be made perfect." The Old Testament gave us our foundation, but God gave us something better: Jesus!

What was the Church of the Old Testament? It was the Church in the wilderness and the Church in the temple that were centered around the slain sacrificial lamb. As we have seen, the lamb is a figure which represents Jesus—and where Jesus is found, we also find victory and revelation! It is only fitting that Pisces should reveal our foundation of the Old Covenant, by which we have become the "seed of Abraham" by faith!

Look at these examples of God's timing with which He revealed His ultimate power and wisdom:

I Kings 18 tells the story of Elijah and the prophets of Baal on Mount Carmel. There, Elijah instructed the prophets of

Baal to kill a bullock, place it upon wood, and call Baal's fire down upon it for sacrifice.

Elijah prepared another bullock in the same manner, but allowed the prophets of Baal to try to call their false god's fire down first. The prophets tried to call the fire all day and even began screaming and cutting themselves, but they could get no results:

> "...Elijah mocked them, and said, Cry aloud: for he is a god; either he is talking, or he is pursuing, or he is in a journey, or peradventure he sleepeth, and must be awaked" (I Kings 18:27).

But when Elijah called down God's fire, God showed Himself as the mighty One Whose timing is perfect:

> "And it came to pass, when midday was past, and they prophesied until **the time of the offering of the evening sacrifice,** that there was neither voice, nor any to answer, nor any that regarded. And it came to pass **at the time of the offering of the evening sacrifice,** that Elijah the prophet came near, and said, Lord God of Abraham, Isaac and of Israel, let it be known this day that thou art God in Israel, and that I am thy servant and that I have done all these things at thy word. Then the fire of the Lord fell, and consumed the burnt sacrifice, and the wood, and the stones, and the dust, and licked up the water that was in the trench" (I Kings 18:29,36,38).

The fire fell at exactly the time of the evening sacrifice, at the time of the Lamb!

In Joshua 7, the children of Israel were badly beaten by the men of Ai, and Joshua was extremely upset over it. How could they have won the battle at Jericho, and lost at Ai? Joshua fell on his face and cried out, "God, what are You going to do? Run us out here and kill us all off? What's the matter with You, God?" He prayed until evening, at the time of the sacrifice of the lamb, and God spoke to him and said, "Get up, Joshua, I want to tell you something." Then, God gave him a revelation of victory which was centered around the sacrificial lamb!

Daniel went on a long fast to receive an answer from God:

> "And I set my face unto the Lord God, to seek by prayer and supplications, with fasting, and sackcloth, and ashes:" (Daniel 9:3).

He said, "God, I have to hear from heaven! I have to know what to do!" And God answered Daniel:

> "Yea, whiles I was speaking in prayer, even the man Gabriel, whom I had seen in the vision at the beginning, being caused to fly swiftly, touched me about the time of the evening oblation. And he informed me and talked with me, and said, O Daniel, I am now come forth to give thee skill and understanding" (Daniel 9:21,22).

Where was victory and revelation from God found in all of these passages? It was found and developed from the sacrificial lamb—the center of the Old Testament Church. How much more should the New Testament church center their vision around God's perfect Sacrificial Lamb, Jesus Christ?

In the pages of the Old Testament, we have been given one

figure after another of Jesus, seen in types and shadows:

> "For the law having a shadow of good things
> to come, and not the very image of the things,
> can never with those sacrifices which they
> offered year by year continually make the
> comers thereunto perfect" (Hebrews 10:1).

In this passage, God is saying, "The Old Covenant isn't enough, because it can only cover up men's sins, but it can't change them." It became plain to see that what we needed was more than forgiveness—we needed new spirits, new natures with which to serve God in a perfect way. Jesus Christ provided us with a new and better way, when he fulfilled the Old Covenant and gave us a new one:

> "Then said he, Lo, I come to do thy will, O
> God. He taketh away the first, that he may
> establish the second. By the which will we are
> sanctified through the offering of the body of
> Jesus Christ once for all" (Hebrews 10:9,10).

The two fish, although swimming in opposite directions, are both held together in the band of the lamb's arm. Christ did not come to break the law of the Old Testament, but He fulfilled it; Pisces describes to us that fulfillment!

In John 15:5, Jesus said, "...Without me ye can do nothing." In the constellation of Pisces, we Christians see ourselves tied together and girded up by the hand of the Lord: "Behold, the Lord God will come with strong hand, and his arms shall rule for him: behold, his reward is with him, and his work before him" (Isaiah 40:10).

The picture of the band being guided by the lamb's arm brings to mind a picture which is found in a prophecy of Isaiah:

"...I will uphold thee with the right hand of my righteousness" (Isaiah 41:10).

How does He uphold us? In love! How are we being guided? In love! How will the Lamb, Jesus Christ, bring together the completeness of the treasures of New and Old? Through His Spirit of love! The band which joins the two fish together is representative of Jesus' beautiful, peaceful Spirit of love.

I can see the love of God shown toward the Church in the next figure, which is a man called **Cepheus,** meaning "the royal branch." You saw Jesus shown as the Branch in Virgo, which fulfilled many prophecies about **how** he would fulfill God's plan. Now in Cepheus, you can see the Branch's relationship to those whom He redeemed.

Notice that as the royal branch, Cepheus holds a sceptre in his hand, and bears a crown of stars upon his head. Crowns are often mentioned in the Bible and we Believers can wear many different ones: 1) I Thessalonians 2:19 speaks of a crown of rejoicing; 2) 2 Timothy 4:8 shows a crown of righteousness; 3) James 1:12 tells of a crown of life; and I Peter 5:4 gives the crown of glory from the Chief Shepherd Himself—Jesus!

When Jesus returns, He will wear more than one crown:

"And I saw heaven opened, and behold a white horse; and he that sat upon him was called Faithful and True, and in righteousness he doth judge and make war. His eyes were as a flame of fire, and on his head were many crowns; and he had a name written, that no man knew, but he himself" (Revelation 19:11,12).

According to the book, **Witness of the Stars,** by Bolinger,

Cepheus has an Egyptian name which means "this one cometh to rule." In his shoulder is a star which is "the quickly returning," and I know that this name quickens your spirit! In Cepheus' girdle is another star, **Al Phirk,** "the redeemer." Cepheus' right knee bears another star, which means "the shepherd." This kingly constellation shows, not the quiet Lamb Who "openeth not his mouth" as pictured in Isaiah 53. Rather, we see Jesus as the righteous Son of God Who will be returning in great power and glory. He won't come as a Lamb, but as our King of kings and Lord of lords!

The book of Job is considered by many to be the oldest book of the Bible, and here an interesting prophecy occurs:

> "For I know that my redeemer liveth, and that
> he shall stand at the latter day upon the
> earth:" (Job 19:25).

David also prophecied of Jesus as his redeemer:

> "Let the words of my mouth, and the medita-
> tion of my heart, be acceptable in thy sight, O
> Lord, my strength, and my redeemer" (Psalm
> 19:14).

Isaiah, too, spoke of the future redeemer of Israel, and our Savior of the world:

> "Thus saith the Lord the King of Israel, and
> his redeemer, the Lord of hosts; I am the first
> and I am the last; and beside me there is no
> God" (Isaiah 44:6).

In fact, Isaiah spoke of his redeemer twelve more times! And throughout the ages, those who place their trust in God have been called the "redeemed" of the Lord. We are His, and therefore He has redeemed us from sin and eternal death!

The last figure in Pisces is **Andromeda,** a picture of the persecuted church, and her name means "the broken down," "the chained," and "the weak." This is a picture of the Church which is not only unpopular with the world, but one which also does not realize the power in being redeemed of the Lord!

In this figure, I see that the world persecutes Andromeda because the devil wants to do everything within his power to hinder the story of Jesus' redemption. To the devil, whose death is already sealed, a church which moves in power of redemption becomes a dangerous weapon!

When I looked more closely at Andromeda's picture on the star map, I noticed that her arms are shown as having broken loose; even though the devil tried to chain her and weaken her, he cannot keep her in bonds. Why? Because God has built His Church upon the Rock—the Word made flesh, Jesus Christ! And when Christians get hold of the Word of God, nothing can hold them down.

In Matthew 16, Jesus asked Peter, "Who do you say that I am?" Then when Peter answered with the Word of God, Jesus replied with a powerful answer:

> "Blessed art thou, Simon Barjona: for flesh and blood hath not revealed it unto thee, but my Father which is in heaven. And I say also unto thee, That thou art Peter, and upon his rock I will build my church; and the gates of hell shall not prevail against it" (Matthew 16:17b, 18).

Jesus said, "The Word gives revelation knowledge of God which the gates of hell cannot prevail against!" Andromeda is breaking loose of her chains.

Colossians 1:27 says that "Christ in you, [is] the hope of glory." Why? Because Christ is the "Word, and the Word was with God, and the Word was God." It is Jesus Christ, the Word of God made Flesh Who became the Lamb of God to obtain our redemption!

It is so great that when the Israelites left Egypt, no one among them was sick or weak; not even their clothing or their shoes wore out! Imagine such a crowd: a million people of all ages, every one of them **healthy!** The Lord dealt with me on the subject and said, "The reason for their health is that they were full of lamb!" They had just eaten the Passover Lamb, the symbol of Jesus Christ! The Israelites had lamb on the outside (the blood upon their doors), and they had lamb on the inside (which they had eaten). Jesus wants to do more than surround you with His presence—He wants to fill you up and be your hope of glory!

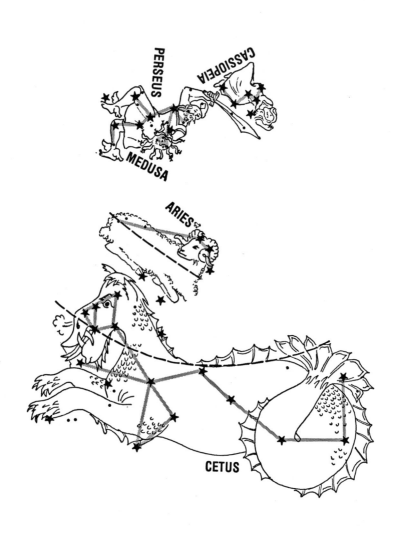

CHAPTER EIGHT
ARIES

As we begin our study of this sign, let's look at Revelation 5:12, which gives us a clear overall view of the sign of Aries:

> "Saying with a loud voice, Worthy is the Lamb that was slain to receive power, and riches, and wisdom, and strength, and honour, and glory, and blessing."

In **Aries** you will see the picture of Jesus as our sacrifice Lamb, yet reigning as our great High Priest over His Body, the Church. The four symbols in Aries are:

1. Aries: the Ram;
2. Cassiopeia: the Woman;
3. Cetus: the Sea Monster; and
4. Perseus: the Warrior or Hero.

The first star immediately gives us a figure of Jesus as the sacrifice Lamb, who was elevated on the cross between heaven and earth. The literal meaning of **Aries** is: "high" or "elevated."

In this constellation there are three principal stars whose names are also very appropriate to the sign of Aries: 1) **El Nath** means "the wounded"; 2) **El Natick** means "the bruised"; 3) **Al Sharetan** means "the slain." The names of these stars make me wonder how people who studied the stars 2,000 years ago could have not recognized Jesus as their sacrifice Lamb Who was slain before the foundation of the world!

Jesus said that He will come back as our King of kings, and as the Lion of the tribe of Judah. Yet before Jesus could return as a Conqueror, He first had to suffer and die as a man:

> "For though he was crucified through weakness, yet he liveth by the power of God..." (II Corinthians 13:4).

> "...But made himself of no reputation, and took upon him the form of a servant, and was made in the likeness of men: And being found in fashion as a man, he humbled himself, and became obedient unto death, even the death of the cross. Wherefore God also hath highly exalted him, and given him a name which is above every name: That at the name of Jesus every knee should bow, of things in heaven, and things in earth, and things under the earth; and that every tongue should confess that Jesus Christ is Lord, to the glory of God the Father" (Philippians 2:7-11).

Jesus died in the form of human weakness—but He will return as Christ, the triumphant King, the anointed One of God.

Cassiopeia is another figure in this constellation. Shown as a queenly elegant woman, she is seated with her foot and chair upon the Arctic Circle: a branch of victory in one hand as she combs her hair with the other. Nearby, the king, Cepheus from the sign of Pisces, extends his scepter toward her. This portrays the Bride, the Lamb's wife being chosen by our Lord and King, Jesus. Revelation 19:7 describes this long-awaited event:

> "Let us be glad and rejoice, and give honour
> to him: for the marriage of the Lamb is come,
> and his wife hath made herself ready."

This picture vividly reminds us of the love story which is found in the book of Esther. In it, King Ahasueras extended his sceptre to his new bride, Esther, to grant permission for her to make a request:

> And it was so when the king saw Esther the
> queen standing in the court, that she obtained
> favour in his sight: and the king held out to
> Esther the golden sceptre that was in his
> hand. So Esther drew near, and touched the
> top of the sceptre" (Esther 5:2).

One of the stars in the constellation of Cassiopeia is called "the freed," and we can parallel this to how Esther turned to God in prayer and fasting, and ultimately obtained the freedom that she desired for her people. If we remember to turn to our King, in troubled times, we will be the "freed ones," also. In our last constellation we saw Andromeda, the Church breaking free of religious bondage. Now Cassiopeia represents the Church who is Spirit-filled: at rest in the Spirit of God.

The next decan of the sign of Aries is **Cetus,** the leviathan; he is a very strange-looking sea monster whose principal star, **Mira** means "Rebel." The characteristic of Cetus' principal star is that it shines brightly, but fades quickly—just as the rebellious Lucifer exalted himself to shine brightly, he faded quickly when God cast him from the heavens. Another star, "the arch-deceiver" foretells of the day when Satan will be made impotent and powerless forever:

> "In that day the Lord with his sore and great and strong sword shall punish leviathan the piercing serpent, even leviathan that crooked serpent; and he shall slay the dragon that is in the sea" (Isaiah 27:1).

Notice how large Cetus is, compared to his conqueror: Satan may try to puff himself up and act overpowering as a monster, but Jesus has already defeated him! Just remember, "...greater is He that is in you than he that is in the world" (I John 4:4).

Now notice that the cord which is held by the ram, between the two Piscean fishes, also goes to the creature. Jesus not only controls the Church—He also controls the devil! Jesus has everything in control:

> "...Which he wrought in Christ, when he raised him from the dead, and set him at his own right hand in the heavenly places, Far above all principality, and power, and might, and dominion, and every name that is named, not only in this world, but also in that which is to come: And hath put all things under his feet, and gave him to be the head over all things to the church,..." (Ephesians 1:20-22).

Now look at **Perseus,** the king. Walking on the brightest part of the Milky Way, he is shown wearing a helmet, with wings upon his feet. Perseus means "the breaker," and he symbolizes Jesus Christ as the **Conqueror.**

As the "Breaker," Jesus broke the chains used by Satan to

keep people in sin's bondage. Throughout the Old and New Testament, the Lamb of God is portrayed as the One Who is worthy to break the seven seals in Revelation, the Breaker of apostate nations, and the Breaker of all hindrances and gates which oppress His people.

Over 2,000 years ago, Micah called Israel together in his way:

> "I will surely assemble, O Jacob, all of thee; I will surely gather the remnant of Israel; I will put them together as the sheep of Bozrah, as the flock in the midst of their fold: they shall make great noise by reason of the multitude of men. The breaker is come up before them: they have broken up, and have passed through the gate, and are gone out by it: and their king shall pass before them, and the Lord on the head of them" (Micah 2:12,13).

Near the king's left foot is a star called **Atik,** meaning, "he who breaks." The brightest middle stars in the figure are a sequence called **Al Genib,** "one who carries away," and **Mirfak,** "one who helps." Again, here is the reminder that our Savior came to be our **help** and finally to **carry us away** in His second coming!

A serpent's head is held in the king's hand, and the serpent is named **Medusa.** The meaning of his name is "the trodden under foot," which explains exactly the symbology which the Bible uses to describe Jesus' defeat over Satan. Especially in the Epistles of the New Testament, we are repeatedly told that Jesus has total dominion, and that all things are **under His feet.** The principal star in the serpent's head has a very ugly name, **Al Ghoul,** and it certainly describes him—I know that you'll agree. The name means "the evil spirit." This star openly reveals Satan's true, dead spiritual nature, a nature of sin. But what does the Scripture have to say about evil spirits?

> "Behold, I give unto you power to tread on
> serpents and scorpions, and over all the
> power of the enemy: and nothing shall by any
> means hurt you" (Luke 10:19).

In the sign of Aries, you have seen Jesus' human weakness becoming divine strength through His perfect submission to God as the sacrifice Lamb. Then you have seen His Church as "the freed one," and walking in the rest of the Spirit of God. Perseus is shown as the breaker of all bondage over Christians, and the one who has trodden the evil one underfoot.

But the most exciting part is that we can walk in the victory of having our names written in the Lamb's book of life! Because He is King, you reign as a king in Him—and you can walk in His authority. Why? Ephesians 1:22-23 tells of God's vision for the Body of Christ, the Church:

> "...And hath put all things under his feet,
> and gave him to be the head over all things to
> the church, Which is his body, the fulness of
> him that filleth all in all."

The last four signs have been Capricornus, Aquarius, Pisces, and Aries, all of which reveal the relationship between Jesus Christ and His Church. In this grouping of four signs, we have moved progressively from the atonement for our sins, to the outpouring of the Holy Spirit, to the Church as the bride of Christ, and finally to the final binding up of Satan.

By now our story which points to Jesus Christ is still only two-thirds complete, however. We have presently been given the authority of Jesus' name and the power of the Holy Spirit so that Satan's deeds may be bound in our lives. But Jesus has sealed his fate, and he will be completely bound and cast into the lake of fire to burn forever. Then, and only then will the Church walk in total knowledge and freedom of the Holy Spirit—for we will see manifested in ourselves the perfect work of Christ in our glorified bodies.

If the first grouping of four signs tells of the work of Jesus Christ and His redemption of mankind, and the second four signs describe the fruit of His labor—the Church—then I can think of no better way to finish the groupings than with God's righteous judgment and final plan for man.

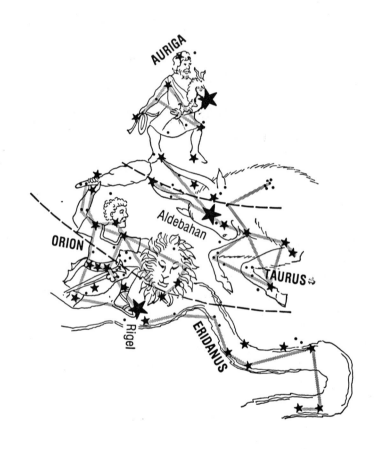

AURIGA

ORION

Aldebahan

TAURUS

Rigel

ERIDANUS

CHAPTER NINE
TAURUS

Taurus begins the last set of four signs in the Zodiac; you will now see the significance of the final "stairs of the ladder," which show the great judgment and conclusion of God's plan for a sinful world.

I thought that this grouping of stars was particularly interesting because the focus is placed on prophecies which are yet to be fulfilled—but could easily come to pass during our lifetime. **Taurus** means "the bull," and he is accompanied by three other symbols which help to tell the story of our Lord's continued work on earth:

1. Taurus: the Bull;
2. Orion: the Hunter;
3. Eridanus: the River; and
4. Auriga: the Shepherd.

Let's look at one of the characteristics of the Bull—his horns. In the Scriptures, there is an animal with one horn on his head, which is called a unicorn. I don't know about you, but I always wondered about those passages. I found that although the unicorn is extinct today, it was once commonly found in Palestine. Psalm 92:10 speaks of this animal:

> "But my horn shalt thou exalt like the horn of
> a unicorn: I shall be anointed with fresh oil."

Psalm 22:21 also shows the unicorn's spiritual significance:

> "Save me from the lion's mouth: for thou hast
> heard me from the horns of the unicorns."

In the Bible, unicorns are described as being strong, mighty animals; and historians claim that they were fierce, wild, and untameable. Numbers 23:22 compares the unicorn's physical might to God's power:

> "God brought them out of Egypt; he hath as it
> were the strength of an unicorn."

If you realize how supernaturally God delivered His people from the hand of the oppressing Egyptians, then you know that this comparison depicts the unicorn as being unusually strong!

Unicorns are also called **reems,** which also mean "a one-horned animal." From the oxen family, unicorns must have had ferocious personalities. Remains of them have been discovered in Israel at certain archaeological sites; but there are not only horns on their heads—they also have horns on their toes! Even though you have probably always seen the unicorn pictured with only one horn, this point has been debated. In our ancient drawing, you will see him illustrated as possessing two horns. The book of Job further describes this controversial creature's undomesticated ways:

> "Will the unicorn be willing to serve thee, or
> abide by thy crib? Canst thou bind the
> unicorn with his band in the furrow? or will he
> harrow the valleys after thee? Wilt thou trust
> him, because his strength is great? or wilt
> thou leave thy labour to him? Wilt thou
> believe him, that he will bring home thy seed,
> and gather it into thy barn?" (Job 39:9-12).

Joseph's two sons are likened to this animal:

> "His glory is like the firstling of his bullock,
> and his horns are like the horns of unicorns:
> with them he shall push the people together
> to the ends of the earth: and they are the ten
> thousands of Ephraim and they are the
> thousands of Manasseh" (Deuteronomy
> 33:17).

Who is this unicorn representing? Fierce and ferocious, yet an animal of servitude—he represents the many-faceted personality of Jesus Christ! You see, Jesus' fierceness has terrorized the devil's kingdom, from which he stole away the keys of death and hell. But to us, Jesus was God's humble Servant Who serves us with the horn of His Own anointing.

The star in the eye of Taurus is called **Aloebaran,** meaning "the leader." The seven stars in his neck make up a constellation which is called **Pleiades.** In the Revelation of John, you see what those stars represent:

> "And I turned to see the voice that spake with
> me. And being turned I saw seven golden
> candlesticks; And in the midst of the seven
> candlesticks one like unto the Son of Man,
> clothed with a garment down to the foot, and
> girt about the paps with a golden girdle. His
> head and his hairs were white like wool, as
> white as snow; and his eyes were as a flame of
> fire; And his feet like unto fine brass, as if they
> burned in a furnace; and his voice as the
> sound of many waters. And he had in his right
> hand seven stars: and out of his mouth went a
> sharp two-edged sword: and his countenance
> was as the sun shineth in his strength"
> (Revelation 1:12-16).

It may be hard for you to imagine Jesus as being fierce, but remember that although He was first born into the world as a gentle Lamb, He will return as the King of kings. In the world's conclusion, the Lamb's wrath shall be poured out in judgment upon the earth:

> [And every free man] ". . .said to the mountains and rocks, Fall on us, and hide us from the face of him that sitteth on the throne, and from the wrath of the Lamb:. . ." (Revelation 6:16).

Christians will not experience this wrath, for I Thessalonians 5:9 says that we have not been appointed unto wrath, but that we have been redeemed by Christ's victory over Satan.

Books, tapes and sermons have proclaimed the terrible times that are in store for the United States and for the whole world. But remember that during the end times two things will occur in a parallel fashion: 1) God will pour judgment out upon those who are sinful and 2) He will **bless** the saints, as prophesied in Joel:

> "Be glad then, ye children of Zion, and rejoice in the Lord your God: for he hath given you the former rain moderately, and he will cause to come down for you the rain, the former rain, and the latter rain in the first month. And the floors shall be full of wheat, and the fats shall overflow with wine and oil. . . .And it shall come to pass afterward, that I will pour out my spirit upon all flesh; and your sons and your daughters shall prophesy, your old men shall dream dreams, your young men shall see visions: And also upon the servants and upon

the handmaids in those days will I pour out
my spirit" (Joel 2:23,24,28,29).

This is God's promise to His saints, not to the world. The
blessing for you will be the outpouring of His Spirit. The flow
of the Holy Spirit is often compared to **water;** therefore, we
can expect a **flood** of God's blessings. He said that He would
pour out His spirit upon "all flesh," so we can expect to see
an ever-increasing revival, when more and more people
receive Christ as their Lord.

We see people getting afraid and hung up about the days
which are ahead; they say, "I'm worried about famine!" And I
often hear Christians talking about building up reserves of
food and water in their store rooms, but the Scriptures never
taught us to do that, did they?

You say, "What about Joseph's dream of the famine?"

Well, who stored up the food? The Israelites or the Egyp-
tians? The Egyptians. But who ate it? Both! Never fear, for
God will never forsake those who are righteous in Christ
Jesus.

Throughout the Scriptures, whenever you see a famine,
you never find God's people going to the basement and digging out the supplies that they've hoarded for the past ten
years! Instead, they put their trust in God; in fact, you almost
always see them **giving** during famines, not hoarding:

"And there stood up one of them named
Agabus, and signified by the Spirit that there
should be great dearth throughout all the
world: which came to pass in the days of
Claudius Caesar. Then the disciples, every
man according to his ability, determined to
send relief unto the brethren which dwelt in
Judaea:" (Acts 11:28-29).

In this passage of Scripture, when Agabus prophesied about an upcoming famine, what was the first action on the part of the disciples? They immediately made plans to send relief to those who would otherwise suffer. They certainly did not start storing up food! God's plan is always for His people to be givers, and by so doing they will never lack for any need. Give without the fear of tomorrow—and you'll always have more than enough.

When you see God's wrath poured out in judgment, remember that this is the penalty for those who have not accepted Christ as Savior—and have thereby rejected Him. Jesus says that if you aren't for Him, you are against Him. The first thing that the enemy wants Christians to think is, "Oh, maybe I won't be caught up in the second coming! Maybe I'll deny Jesus and take the Antichrist's mark!" Don't even think that. The Bible clearly states that you have not been appointed to wrath, but rather to redemption, praise the Lord!

The mighty hunter in this series of figures speaks of how Jesus will redeem His Own, for the star's name is **Orion,** which means "He who cometh forth as light." Will Jesus come forth as light? He will, according to Matthew 24:27:

"For as the lightning cometh out of the east,
and shineth even unto the west; so shall also
the coming of the Son of man be."

From Orion's starry belt hangs a sword, and its handle has the figure of a lamb upon it. This sword is a symbol of the Lamb of God, Who was the Word made flesh. In the Old Testament, both Job and Amos spoke of this hunter, Orion. Job 38:31 questions the power of man in the presence of One so great:

"Canst thou bind the sweet influences of

Pleiades, or loose the bands of Orion?"

Remember that Pleiades is the constellation of seven stars which are formed about the neck of the unicorn. This is very exciting to me, because Job has referenced both of these starry sequences, and tied them together. Again, the Lord reveals in His Word that the story in the heavens in His alone.

Who can loose the bands of Orion? No one can! The Lord will accomplish that which He has declared in His Word, as confirmed by the star called **Betalguese,** which means "the branch coming." In his foot shines **Rigel,** "the foot that crusheth."

Now look at the three bright stars in the girdle of Orion, which are called "the three kings." Every constellation on the map of stars has corresponding Scripture and the one which speaks of Orion's girdle is found in Isaiah 11:5: "And righteousness shall be the girdle of his loins, and faithfulness the girdle of his reins." Finally, notice the star which is found in the left breast of Orion, **Bellatrix;** its name means "swiftly coming."

When you think of Jesus quickly returning, what do you imagine will happen to this earth afterward? We all know that the next event in God's plan will be the years of tribulation, and I find this in the series of stars which is called "the river of the judge," flowing east and west and then into the underworld.

At first, I wondered why a river would flow into hell. I found the answer in a passage of Scripture in Isaiah 30. Notice the contrast between the fate of those who are saved, and those who are damned, and upon whom God's wrath will descend:

"Behold, the name of the Lord cometh from far, burning with his anger, and the burden thereof is heavy: his lips are full of indignation, and his tongue, as a devouring fire: And his breath, as an overflowing stream, shall reach to the midst of the neck, to sift the nations with the sieve of vanity: and there shall be a bridle in the jaws of the people, causing them to err.

Ye shall have a song, as in the night when a holy solemnity is kept: and gladness of heart as when one goeth with a pipe to come into the mountain of the Lord, to the mighty One of Israel. And the Lord shall cause his glorious voice to be heard, and shall shew the lightning down of his arm, with the indignation of his anger, and with the flame of a devouring fire, with scattering, and tempest, and hailstones. For through the voice of the Lord shall the Assyrian be beaten down, which smote with a rod. And in every place where the grounded staff shall pass, which the Lord shall lay upon him, it shall be with tabrets and harps: and in battles of shaking will he fight with it. For Tophet is ordained of old; yea, for the king it is prepared; he hath made it deep and large: the pile thereof is fire and much wood; the breath of the Lord, like a stream of brimstone, doth kindle it" (Isaiah 30:27-33).

This "stream of brimstone" was also prophesied in the book of Daniel:

"I beheld till the thrones were cast down, and the Ancient of days did sit, whose garment was white as snow, and the hair of his head like the pure wool: his throne was like the fiery flame, and his wheels as burning fire. A fiery stream issued and came forth from before him: thousand thousands ministered unto him, and ten thousand times ten thousand stood before him: the judgment was set, and the books were opened.

I beheld them because of the voice of the great words which the horn spake: I beheld even till the beast was slain, and his body destroyed, and given to the burning flame" (Daniel 7:9-11).

This river must end in the lake of fire and brimstone which was prophesied by John and recorded in the book of Revelation:

"And death and hell were cast into the lake of fire. This is the second death. And whosoever was not found written in the book of life was cast into the lake of fire" (Revelation 20:14,15).

God never intended that mankind should spend eternity in a place which was originally created for the devil and his angels. Hell was not made for you, but He desires to have your name in the Lamb's book of life, so that you may spend eternity with God. Aren't you glad that you are in the book of Life? Jesus Himself told us, "That's a reason to rejoice!"

So far, Taurus may appear to be an extremely ferocious, strong series of figures. However, the final series of stars ends this sign on a very sweet and merciful note. The last figure in Taurus is a Shepherd who is occupied with caring for his flock. In Latin, the shepherd's name is **Auriga,** and it means "the conductor of the reigns." Jesus, our Good Shepherd, is looking after His flock as tenderly as always.

Notice that a mother goat is resting in the crook of His arm, and He holds the figure of a baby goat in His hand. Then see the band which he carries, resembling a ribbon. Jesus is the One Who guides and leads His people, and at the same time, binds the works of the enemy. I think that God is saying, "I don't want Christians to worry about the end times; I want them to know that I am merciful toward them." In the midst of fiery wrath God continually extends mercy, mercy, mercy towards His people—toward you.

The principal star in the shepherd's figure is called **Capella,** translated into "the band of the goats." People have really gotten hung up over this: "Why would I want to be a goat?" But it is God's business to gather up unruly goats and make lambs of them. Jesus, our Scapegoat, identified with us in our sin, so that we could identify with Him in His righteousness.

Why would a shepherd be gathering goats, as well as lambs? Because the outpouring of the Spirit shall be upon "all flesh." In I Corinthians 1:26, the Apostle Paul said, "not many mighty, not many noble are called." Jesus did not come to heal those who imagined themselves to be healthy but to heal those who would confess that they were weak. In the outpouring of His Spirit upon all flesh, you will see many, many "goats," sin-sick people being healed by the mercy of the Good Shepherd. God can turn goats into lambs, and in the final days, many will be drawn to Him.

For years, a great dispute has existed over whether the Holy Spirit will leave the earth when the Church is taken out. Some people use 2 Thessalonians 2:7 to prove their point: ". . . he who now letteth will let, until He be taken out of the way." Many Bible teachers claim that the second "He" is referring to the Holy Spirit, but I seriously doubt that is true! I am positive that the Holy Spirit will have to be present during those times, in light of what the Bible says about the "two witnesses," in Revelation 11:

> "And I will give power unto my two witnesses, and they shall prophesy a thousand two hundred and threescore days, clothed in sackcloth" (Revelation 11:3).

In the same chapter of Revelation; the Lord reveals that these two prophets will be killed and their dead bodies openly displayed in the street for a stretch of three days. Suddenly, in the full view of multitudes worldwide, those two witnesses will miraculously be raised from the dead by God Himself! How can these two witnesses minister to people without the Holy Spirit to help them? (He is, after all, the "Helper.") It would be impossible! The only way that they could witness about Jesus would be through the power of the Holy Spirit.

Revelation 14:6 says that before the seven final plagues are poured upon the earth, an angel will soar through the heavens to proclaim the Gospel to men one last time upon the earth. Again, we see that there will be those who refuse to bow to the Antichrist's lies and will be martyred for their faith.

How will men have the strength to stand in that day? How will men refuse to be swayed by Satan's devices, and "love not their lives unto death?" The righteous will only stand by relying on One Person alone: the indwelling Holy Spirit!

I know that there are people who are fully aware of Jesus' Lordship; yet they intend to be on earth when the Rapture takes place, and they say, "Oh, I'll make it through the tribulation. I don't want to serve God now, but I'll serve Him then." I have one question for those people who say that. "If you cannot serve the Lord now, when it's all up-front and legal, how in the world do you intend to do it in those times of persecution?"

Of course, the Holy Spirit will necessarily be present to strengthen those who do sincerely give their lives to the Lord during that time, both Jews and Gentiles alike. The Bible tells us that a great number of Jews will be converted, literally saying that 12,000 people from each of the twelve tribes, 144,000, will be converted. That is a tremendous number of people, and it would be impossible to draw them near without the Holy Spirit.

You can see that God is showing you that He will even be merciful in His judgment, that He will still be calling lost goats and sheep into the Kingdom.

There are always two simultaneous actions which occur in God's dealing with man: the flow of God's Spirit and the tug of Satan. But we don't have to listen to Satan! We can refuse Him forever and flow according to the Spirit of Love and the Gospel of the Kingdom. I think that Psalm 37:39,40 offers a beautiful promise to end this constellation with:

> "But the salvation of the righteous is of the Lord: he is their strength in the time of trouble. And the Lord shall help them, and deliver them: he shall deliver them from the wicked, and save them, because they trust in him."

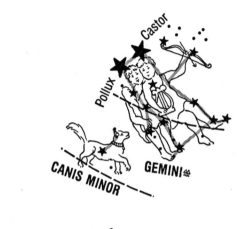

Castor

Pollux

CANIS MINOR

GEMINI

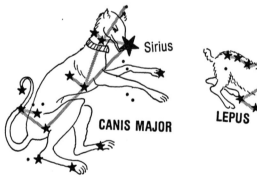

Sirius

CANIS MAJOR

LEPUS

CHAPTER TEN
GEMINI

Gemini presents a heavenly union called "the twins." In it, two figures sit closely together leaning one on another in a loving attitude with their feet resting on the Milky Way. That is Jesus with His left arm securely around you while His other hand is grasping a club with which He protects you from the enemy. This is not a picture of preparation for war but rather rest from the war. Let's get an overview of all of Gemini's figures:

1. Gemini: the Twins;
2. Lepus: the Rabbit;
3. Canis Major: the Large Dog; and
4. Canis Minor: the Small Dog.

The twin who is being cuddled is clasping a harp in one hand, and a bow and arrow in the other. Revelation 14:2 confirms that the redeemed of the Lord will "say so" with the praise of harps:

> "And I heard a voice from heaven, as the voice of many waters, and as the voice of a great thunder: and I heard the voice of harpers harping with their harps:..."

Are those harpers the ones whose names were written in

the Lamb's book of life? I found my answer in Revelation 14:4, which discloses their identity as being "...they which follow the Lamb whithersoever he goeth..." Revelation 5:8 shows the harpers praising the Lion of the tribe of Judah, for He alone is able to open the book which is sealed with seven seals.

> "And I saw as it were a sea of glass mingled with fire: and them that had gotten the victory over the beast, and over his image, and over his mark, and over the number of his name, stand on the sea of glass, having the harps of God. And they sing the song of Moses the servant of God, and the song of the Lamb, saying, Great and marvelous are thy works, Lord God Almighty; just and true are thy ways, Thou King of saints" (Revelation 15:2,3).

The bow and arrow in the small twin's hand is the one which refers to prophecy in Revelation 19:11. In it, the Church has an active role in Christ's triumphant and final return, when He comes riding a great white horse:

> "...and he that sat upon him was called Faithful and True, and in righteousness he doth judge and make war..."

In this return, we His saints will accompany Him:

> "And the armies which were in heaven followed upon white horses, clothed in fine linen, white and clean" (Revelation 19:14).

> "Then shall the Lord go forth, and fight against those nations, as when he fought in the day of battle....And the Lord my God

shall come, and in all the saints with thee"
(Zechariah 14:3,5b).

The loving picture of the twins also represents the "marriage supper of the Lamb." As the Bride of Christ, we will be inseparably united as One with Him. He and His Church, His Body, will be together forever.

Now look at the protective figure: to the south in this left foot is a large star which is named **Al Henal,** meaning "the hurt, the wounded." We cannot get away from the prophecy of Genesis 3:15 in our study of the stars; and this star reminds us that we shall know that Jesus' body bears the mark of Satan's "bruising." We are also reminded that although our Lord was "bruised," Satan was the one who was crushed, for the prominent star in the larger twin's head is called **Pollux,** "the ruler." Revelation 19:15 prophesies about Jesus' Rulership:

> ". . . and he shall rule them with a rod of iron:
> and he treadeth the winepress of the
> fierceness and wrath of Almighty God."

Now notice a star named **Wasat,** which is located at the center of the larger twin's body. This star means "seated," and is a picture of the judgment to come. As a man, Jesus came to serve, to minister to those who would be His Church. Now, His work completed, He is seated at the right hand of God:

> ". . . and upholding all things by the word of
> his power, when he had by himself purged our
> sins, sat down on the right hand of the Majes-
> ty on high" (Hebrews 1:3b).

In the picture of the star named Wasat, we see that Jesus

has already accomplished what He intended to do; His foe has already been defeated, and afterwards, He sat down and said, "You go":

> "Go ye therefore, and teach all nations, bap-
> tizing them in the name of the Father, and of
> the Son, and of the Holy Ghost: Teaching
> them to observe all things whatsoever I have
> commanded you: and, lo, I am with you alway,
> even unto the end of the world" (Matthew
> 28:19-20).

Jesus is with us now, and will be with us forever! We are so close to Him, that He will even bring us with Him to judge the earth, as seen in the next star, **Casore,** which means "the coming ruler." Why is Jesus shown as a "Coming Ruler," in the **"twins"** constellation? Because He will not be returning alone! The Bible even foretells of our being **together** with Christ during His Millenial reign on earth. It explains what our role shall be: He that overcometh shall rule and reign with Him (Revelation 3:21).

I firmly believe that the second figure, symbolizing the Church, has a great part in taking the Kingdom. The fact that the star which is found in the smaller twin's head is called "the coming ruler" reinforces my theory—for it speaks of a return **to rule,** implying that a kingdom will be established, where Jesus' rulership will be set up.

Revelation 21:7 also speaks of overcomers, saying that whoever overcomes will inherit all things. What do you over-come? Primarily, "self." A very young Christian once told me that the Lord said to him, "Take up your cross and follow Me."

He said, "Lord, what is my 'cross'?"

The Lord answered, "Your cross is your ego. All egos belong at the cross."

If you will take your ego to the cross and let it die, then you will live in resurrection life; but if you don't, you'll drag it around all of your life. What are you going to do? It's up to you to make the critical choice.

These decisions which we now endure on earth are those which are preparing us to rule and reign with Him in the Millenial reign of 1,000 years of peace. For any Scriptural task, you will see Scriptural preparation which is continual. Before God gives us an assignment, we must prove that we are responsible enough to handle it:

> "...Well, thou good servant: because thou
> hast been faithful in a very little, have thou
> authority over ten cities" (Luke 19:17).

The above principle is demonstrated in the life of a man named Othniel, whose story is told in the book of Joshua. In it, Caleb said that whoever took Kirjath-sepher, a city inhabited by giants, would not only receive the city, but would also marry his daughter. Why did he say that? Because Caleb wanted a son-in-law of such dedication and love that he would risk his life for her. But Othniel looked ahead and saw the reward, and took on the quest as preliminary training to rule. Later in the book of Judges, we find that he is listed as Israel's first judge! His efforts and reliability paid off.

In an account found in Judges 3:8, we find that the children of Israel did evil in the sight of the Lord, and because of their disobedience, God "sold them into the hands" of Mesopotamia's evil king, Chushan-rishathaim. The children of Israel were his servants for eight years, but finally when they repented and cried unto the Lord, He raised up Othniel to deliver them. Following the leading of the Spirit of God, Othniel "judged Israel and went out to war; and the Lord delivered Chushan-rishathaim into his hands" (Judges 3:10).

The next forty years were a time of rest from war because of a man who leaned on the Holy Spirit for his supply of courage. He was made a judge and protector of Israel because he had esteemed spiritual preparation.

When you spend time in God's Word and time in prayer, your spiritual preparation is very effectual! You are ready for spiritual battle, and I think that the next figure shows what happens when you're fully dressed in God's armor: the set of stars shows a rabbit who is scurrying away, as though in great fear. The rabbit's name is **Lepus,** meaning "the enemy of the coming," and he is fleeing because he fears the power of the Body of Christ, as they walk in the fullness which God intended. The figure of Lepus is hurrying away because he is very frightened of the heavenly union which is depicted in the first decan of Gemini. In the end, Satan and all of his demons who are truly "enemies of the Coming One," will be cast into the Lake of Fire forever."

Another figure in this sign of Gemini is a "large dog" whose name is **Canus Major.** Dogs hunt rabbits, don't they? Obviously, this dog is involved in the hunt, and his principal star's name, **Sirius,** actually means, "prince," or "guardian."

Another star in this constellation is **Nazseirene** (Nazarene), which means "the sent prince." Isaiah prophesied about our Lord's princely role:

> "For unto us a child is born, unto us a son is given: and the government shall be upon his shoulder: and his name shall be called Wonderful, Counsellor, The mighty God, The everlasting Father, The Prince of Peace" (Isaiah 9:6).

The constellation shows Jesus as the One Who is sent to be a Prince for a single reason: to establish everlasting peace between man and God.

Canis Major's small companion is a "little dog" who is

called **Canis Minor,** again depicting a large, protective figure and a small one who is dependent upon him. We are to be completely dependant upon Jesus; all that we have to do is stick with Him like glue, and He will protect us, sending the devil running. The only battle which you must fight is the good fight of faith—and it's a good battle because it's the one that Jesus has won for you! The idea of leaning completely upon Jesus' strength is expressed in Revelation 14:4:

> "These are they which were not defiled with women; for they are virgins. These are they which follow the Lamb whithersoever he goeth."

Just follow Jesus! Follow the Lamb absolutely anywhere that He leads you. I Thessalonians 4:17 deals with the end result of following Him:

> "Then we which are alive and remain shall be caught up together with them in the clouds, to meet the Lord in the air: and so shall we ever be with the Lord."

Gemini shows the outpouring of God's Spirit in the sense that He is coming to receive a Church of glory and praise unto Himself. The devil is on the run, for he knows that his end is near! Most importantly, this sign shows that the Holy Spirit is taking care of the Body of Christ, the Church. It reinforces the Scriptures by showing that it is by the Spirit of God that we may live as one with Christ now—as we will forever!

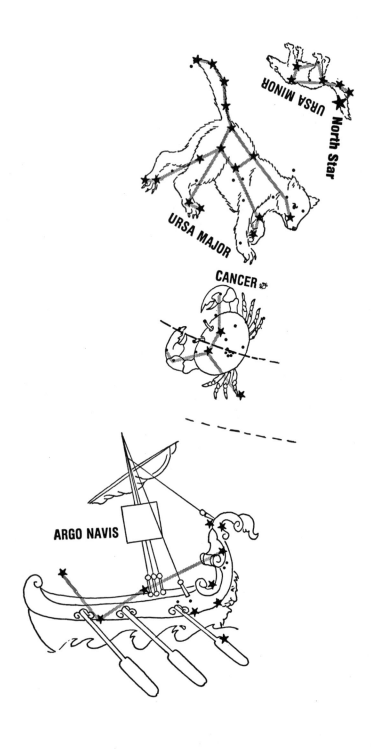

CHAPTER ELEVEN
CANCER

The ultimate fulfillment of God's promise to us through Abraham is found symbolized by the sign of Cancer:

> "That in blessing I will bless thee, and in multiplying I will multiply thy seed as the stars of the heaven, and as the sand which is upon the sea shore; and thy seed shall possess the gate of his enemies;" (Genesis 22:17).

> "Now to Abraham and his seed were the promises made. He saith not, And to seeds, as of many; but as of one, And to thy seed, which is Christ. And if ye be Christ's then are ye Abraham's seed, and heirs according to the promise" (Galatians 3:16,29).

Since the symbol of Cancer happens to be a crab, you may want to know, "How can a crab have anything to do with Jesus Christ, His Church, or the wrath of God?" You will see the significance in this chapter.

The sign of Cancer has four symbols:

1. Cancer: the Crab;
2. Ursa Minor: the Little Bear;
3. Ursa Major: the Large Bear; and
4. Argo Navis: the Ship.

The first significance I saw in the crab is that it is a water-born animal, reminding me of the symbol of a fish; and thus, that the Church also is born of water and of the Spirit. I saw that the many legs of the crab can represent many members in the Body of Christ. If you examine the crab's development and life cycle, you can see a typology between it and the Church. For instance, the shedding of its shell:

> "For we know that if our earthly house of this
> tabernacle were dissolved, we have a building
> of God, an house not made with hands, eter-
> nal in the heavens" (2 Corinthians 5:1).

From one dispensation to another the Church keeps growing. It can be compared to a crab's shedding of its shell and gaining a new one which fits the enlarged body. As the church grows and develops spiritually, from one era to the next, we must "shed our shells" of doctrine and tradition in order to receive the truth of God's Word! We must never let our earthly traditions make the Word of God have no effect in our lives.

Also, this segment of Scripture in 2 Corinthians states that our bodies are "shells" which are physically separating us from being with Christ, although we are with Him by the Spirit. Someday, when Jesus gives a great shout, we will put off our earthly bodies for "glorified" bodies or homes from the heaven:

> "Behold I shew you a mystery; We shall not
> all sleep, but we shall all be changed, In a
> moment, in the twinkling of an eye, at the last
> trump: for the trumpet shall sound, and the
> dead shall be raised incorruptible, and we
> shall be changed. For this incorruptible must
> put on incorruption, and this mortal must put

on immortality. So when this corruptible shall have put on incorruption, and this mortal shall have put on immortality, then shall be brought to pass the saying that is written, Death is swallowed up in victory" (I Corinthians 15:51-54).

In this sign you will see all of the Christians entering their final home after the second coming of Christ, for the word **Cancer** means "rest secured." Jesus has secured a rest for us:

"For we which have believed do enter into rest, as he said, As I have sworn in my wrath, if they shall enter into my rest: although the works were finished from the foundation of the world. . . . And in this place again, if they shall enter into my rest" (Hebrews 4:3,5).

A large cluster of stars appears in the crab's mid-section, and they are called "the beehive." Some historians have called it "the manger." This series of stars are named **Praesepe,** meaning "the multitude," "the offspring," or "innumerable seed." Revelation 7:9,10 explains who this multitude is:

"After this I beheld, and lo, a great multitude which no man could number, of all nations and kindreds, and people and tongues, stood before the throne and before the Lamb, clothed with white robes, and palms in their hands, And cried with a loud voice saying, "Salvation to our God which sitteth upon the throne, and unto the Lamb."

There is a 24-star total in the small constellation of Praesepe, and when I counted them, I found the Scripture in

Revelation 4:4, about the 24 elders:

> "And round about the throne were four and twenty seats: and upon the seats I saw four and twenty elders sitting, clothed in white raiment; and they had on their heads crowns of gold."

In this figure I see the multitudes who are continually shedding their exterior fleshly habits being changed from glory to glory, from faith to faith, and from strength to strength. As we all grow in the security and rest of Jesus Christ, we shed old shells and grow up into Him as we take on more beautiful ways and are finally transformed into His image.

The next of Cancer's decans is that of a small bear, once depicted as a sheepfold, according to Hebrew folklore. His name is **Ursa Minor.** In this constellation you will see seven principal stars, called **Septentriones:** "the seven which turn." You also see that the Polar star is in this constellation.

At one time, the Polar star was located in the curve of Draco's tail. It was at that time that I believe the star's position signified that the earth was in the enemy's possession. Today, that star has traveled far from the dragon's tail to be located in the small "sheepfold." I believe that the movement of this Polar star signifies that the saints are ever moving closer to permanently reigning with the Lord.

Now focus in on **Ursa Major,** the "big bear," and Cancer's next decan. He was recognized in ancient times as the "Great Sheepfold," or the "resting place of the flock." Remember that Cancer means "rest secured," so here we see reinforcement to the rest which is given to His saints.

The star called **Mizar,** on the bear's tail, bears witness to this rest as it is translated to mean "a guarded, enclosed place." When you enter the spiritual rest of God, no enemy can penetrate your fortress (unless you allow it). And when we are eternally with the Lord in our final place of rest, we will certainly have entered the enclosed place of God's protection.

Ursa Major and Ursa Minor are part of the flock which follows Bootes, the Shepherd which is found in the constellation of Virgo. Job knew the stars' names in this set of stars and was aware that they symbolized a **part** of a flock, for he spoke of **Arcturus,** the star in Bootes' knee:

> ". . . canst thou guide Arcturus and his sons?"
> (Job 38:32).

In the Hebrew translation, the word **sons** means "Ash" or "Aish," and this word means "the seven stars of the Great Bear." Job spoke of a connection between the two constellations!

Who else could the seven stars signify? They represent the seven churches which are mentioned in the first chapters of the Revelation of St. John:

> "I was in the Spirit on the Lord's day, and heard behind me a great voice as of a trumpet, Saying I am Alpha and Omega, the first and the last: and, What thou seest, write in a book, and send it unto the seven churches which are in Asia; unto Ephesus, and unto Smyrna, and unto Pergamos, and unto Thyatira, and unto Sardis, and unto Philadelphia, and unto Laodicea" (Revelation 1:10,11).

Cancer shows the flocks of the Good Shepherd being gathered together, just as prophecy has foretold they would.

Paul caught another mystery which is seen in this sign: it is the Jewish reception of Jesus' Messiahship. He spoke of the gathering together in Ephesians 2:14:

> "...For he is our peace, who hath made both
> one, and hath broken down the middle wall of
> partition between us...;"

The final decan shown in Cancer is that of a ship, called **Argo Navis.** Its brightest star is **Caopus,** meaning "the possession of Him Who cometh." In this light Jesus' words in John 14:1-3 become more meaningful:

> "Let not your heart be troubled: ye believe in
> God, believe also in me. In my Father's house
> are many mansions: if it were not so, I would
> have told you. I go to prepare a place for you.
> And if I go and prepare a place for you, I will
> come again, and receive you unto myself; that
> where I am, there ye may be also."

This is a constellation of stars which represents the "ship" of God's people entering Zion's harbor! How can that be? First, examine the facts about Noah's ark, and you shall see the answer.

Noah's ark was constructed with a very special pitch, sealing out all of the cracks so that no flood waters could enter and sink the ship. The Hebrew word for "pitch" really means atonement! The Gospel ship is one which has been sealed with the atoning blood of God's Son, Jesus Christ. It is to seal off the contamination of living in a sinful world. Jesus has sealed our rest with "supernatural pitch"—His blood.

The ark only had one window in it, and the window was located in the ceiling of the ship's upper story. Noah's family was unable to look out of the ark's sides to view the world's destruction; they could only look up. Like those who were in the ark, so we should only look up—for our deliverance!

Today, we are a part of the Gospel ark. Many pressures are coming against the presentation of God's Word to the world but we can be sure that our safety, our rest, is secure now and forever. Jesus Himself is our safe Harbor.

What is Argo Navis carrying? I think that it is filled with a multitude of crabs; and the one thing they have in common is their shell which has been completely transformed! Mortality has taken on immortality in the image of Jesus Christ. The Bible tells us that when we see Him, we shall be like Him!

Isn't this sign a blessed hope? Cancer, the crab, encourages and reminds us that transformation is at hand; and the word for transformation actually means "transfiguration." Just as Jesus shone and radiated God's glory on the Mount of Transfiguration, here we see ourselves as God's multitudes of **lights** to the world—radiating His light, and being transfigured, just as Jesus was.

This is the sign which prepares and summons us to be ready for that moment which will come like a "twinkling of an eye," when we will join our Lord of Glory!

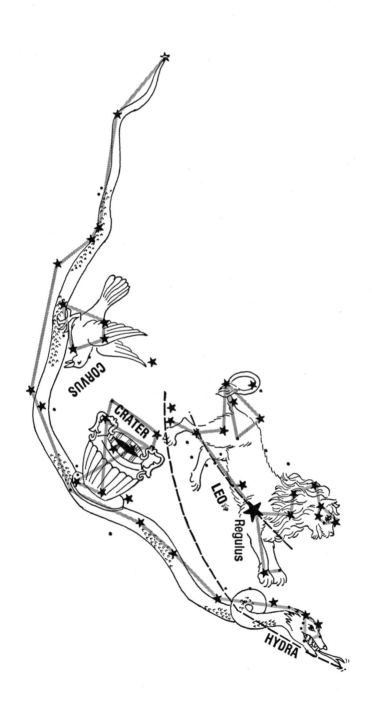

CHAPTER TWELVE
LEO

You started the study of Signs in the Heavens with Virgo because you had to first see Jesus as the Seed of woman Who would bruise Satan's head. Now you have seen how the stars portray His fulfillment of those prophecies and His work within the church. Leo, our final sign, will depict Jesus' reign as the King. Leo means "lion," and so you will see Jesus operating in full power and strength as the exalted Lion of the tribe of Judah. The four signs in Leo are:

1. Leo: the Lion;
2. Hydra: the Water Snake;
3. Crater: the Cup of Wrath; and
4. Corvus: the Raven.

Revelation 5:5 shows Jesus' action as the Lion of the tribe of Judah:

> "...Weep not: behold, the Lion of the tribe of Judah, the Root of David, hath prevailed to open the book, and to loose the seven seals thereof."

A lion is, of course, described in the Bible as being the mightiest of all other animals:

"A lion which is strongest among beasts, and turneth not away for any" (Proverbs 30:30).

Regulus is one of Leo's principal stars, and its meaning is "the feet which crush." Jesus' feet crushed Satan, but so did yours:

"Behold, I give unto you power to tread on serpents and scorpions, and over all the power of the enemy: and nothing shall by any means hurt you" (Luke 10:19).

No demon in hell could stop you from receiving Jesus' salvation for you from the wages of sin. Likewise, no demon in hell can have power over your life as a member of the Body of Christ. All things are under His feet, and you are in Him. Thus, all things are under your feet, too! Jesus is truly All Powerful, for while He gives of His strength and power to you to use against the enemy, His Own power is never diminished at all. This is His position as the Lion!

In this constellation you discover that the Lion of Judah is preparing to crush his foe's head and eternally seal his destruction. The enemy is represented by Hydra, the water snake. Psalm 91:13 describes Hydra:

"Thou shalt tread upon the lion and the adder: the young lion and dragon thou shalt trample under foot."

Another star in the body of Leo is one which surely shakes the gates of hell, as Satan awaits only doom. The star is called **Denebola,** and it means "the Lord Who cometh with haste." Sin runs rampant in this world, and it has since the curse was put on it as recorded in Genesis. Yet Christians aren't to be swayed by the sin. We are only to be moved to spread the

Gospel in the short time before the end arrives. Every day in which another soul receives Christ as Lord and Savior is another day of God's mercy, for it is not His will that any should perish.

The third star in this constellation is called **Al Giebha,** and I found that its name adds still another dimension to the picture of Jesus as the Lion. It means "the exalted." Centuries ago Isaiah prophesied, "Thou art my God and I will exalt thee" (Isaiah 25:1). Now we see the prophecy fulfilled.

To me, one of the most interesting stars in the constellation of the lion is **Mincher Al Asad,** which predicts "the punishing or tearing of him who lays waste." Does the devil lay waste? You know that he does! This star tells that his future is certain, and his days are numbered. The Lion of Judah is going to punish the one who has been a thief and liar.

Genesis 8:9 gives a prophecy of Jacob's, in which he foretold the triumph of the Lion of the tribe of Judah. This prophecy occurred when he was blessing the tribe of Judah:

> "Judah, thou art he whom thy brethren shall praise: thy hand shall be in the neck of thine enemies; thy father's children shall bow down before thee. Judah is a lion's whelp: from the prey, my son, thou art gone up: he stooped down, he couched as a lion, and as an old lion; who shall rouse him up?" (Genesis 49:8,9).

This is the very beginning of the nation of Israel, and Jacob is prophesying about Messiah! He knew that the Lion would win, and that the devil would be destroyed and laid to waste.

The prophet Hosea also prophesied about Jesus as a Lion·

"Therefore I will be unto them as a lion; as a

leopard by the way will I observe them: I will
meet them as a bear that is bereaved of her
whelps, and will rend the caul of their heart,
and there will I devour them like a lion: the
wild beast shall tear them" (Hosea 13:7,8).

In Leo, the serpent has finally been cast from the earth and
is thrown into the fiery pit. The mission of the seed of a
woman was to bruise Satan's head, and the mission is accomplished. But in Revelation we see that first there is war:

"And the dragon was wroth with the woman,
and went to make war with the remnant of her
seed, which keep the commandments of God,
and have the testimony of Jesus Christ"
(Revelation 12:17).

Looking at his picture it appears as though Hydra covers
nearly one third of the star map doesn't it? He has always
tried to convince mankind that he was king, conqueror and
god of the world. Unfortunately, many have been deceived by
his lies, not desiring to know God's truth. But God has said
that He alone is true, even if it makes every man a liar! Hydra
may make himself look big, but in the end when people see
him in the pit, they'll be amazed at how a pitful one like Satan
could have deceived the nations!

The book of Revelation tells of his pending and certain
doom:

"And the great dragon was cast out, that old
serpent, called the Devil, and Satan, which
deceiveth the whole world: he was cast out into the earth, and his angels were cast out with
him. And I heard a loud voice saying in
heaven, Now is come salvation, and strength,

and the kingdom of our God, and the power
of his Christ: for the accuser of our brethren
is cast down, which accursed them before our
God day and night" (Revelation 12:9,10).

The interesting cup which rests upon Hydra's back is
named **Crater,** and it really appears as though it is ready to
tip over. Crater is representative of God's vengeance and
wrath upon unrighteousness, and it is seen right where it
belongs: on Satan's back. Psalm 75:8 describes the scene of
Crater:

> "For in the hand of the Lord there is a cup,
> and the wine is red; it is full of mixture; and he
> poureth out of the same: but the dregs
> thereof, all the wicked of the earth shall wring
> them out, and drink them."

Undoubtedly Hydra sees the Lion of Judah in close pursuit,
but is unable to move quickly because of the cup of God's
wrath upon his back. Psalm 11:6 elaborates on the cup of
God's wrath:

> "Upon the wicked he shall rain snares, fire
> and brimstone, and an horrible tempest: this
> shall be the portion of their cup."

At last the Lion of the tribe of Judah settles the final score
with His enemy! The final vengeance is shown in the next
sign, **Corvus,** "the raven." The raven is a bird of destruction
and punishment. It is a bird of God's wrath, and this is shown
in the Scriptures:

> "The eye that mocketh at his father, and
> despiseth to obey his mother, the ravens of

the valley shall pick it out, and the young eagles shall eat it" (Proverbs 30:17).

"This day will the Lord deliver thee into mine hand; and I will smite thee, and take thine head from thee; and I will give the carcasses of the host of the Philistines this day unto the fowls of the air, and to the wild beasts of the earth; that all the earth may know that there is a God in Israel" (I Samuel 17:46).

As birds which signify God's wrath, ravens will be participants in the battle of Armegeddon:

"And I saw an angel standing in the sun; and he cried with a loud voice, saying to all the fowls that fly in the midst of heaven, Come and gather yourselves together unto the supper of the great God; that ye may eat the flesh of kings, and the flesh of captains, and the flesh of mighty men, and the flesh of horses, and of them that sit on them, and the flesh of all men, both free and bond, both small and great" (Revelation 19:17,18).

At the end of this sign you see God causing His creatures of the air to accomplish His will. Leo, the Lion of the tribe of Judah, comes as a conqueror and leads the armies of God to defeat the "old dragon" in the weary earth's final battle. Justice has been completed.

SUMMARY

From now on when someone mentions astrology to you, just let them know that you're already aware of what the stars represent. You can tell the person, "God placed them as signs in the heavens, and they have always pointed men toward His Son, Jesus Christ."

It is obvious to me that Satan would never want mankind to see such words as "redemption" written in the sky. But I have told you the story of redemption which was seen by Job as he looked upon the signs in the heavens.

Let God's story in the stars show you His truth. I hope that every time you look into the heavens that you will see God's truth in everything. Best of all, you can beat Satan at his own game: you can share the Lord's story with all the people you know.

1. The Redeemer

Virgo: The Seed of woman is the "Desired One" with a nature that has two parts: He is both Son of man and Son of God. He is the exalted Shepherd and Harvester.

Libra: Jesus paid the price to save us from our sin: He died on the cross as a sacrifice for us. What happened? The scales of justice which were once "the price deficient" have become "the price that covers" our sins. We have been given Christ's righteousness before God.

Scorpio: On the cross, Satan stung Jesus with the poison of sin. Nevertheless, Jesus crushed him and triumphed over him in our behalf. He won the victory over the oppression of sin and death. Now we need never to experience the sting of any death, physical, spiritual or eternal.

Sagittarius: The Archer Who is seen as Son of man and Son of God promises that He will return to the earth again to claim His people unto Himself. The catching away of His bride, the Church, is seen in Christ's second return, brought about by Christians worshipping God. Finally, we see the dragon's gloomy future when he will be cast into the lake of fire.

2. People

Capricornus: Jesus' atonement brings forth a new Church Who are set apart to shine as priests to nations. Deliverance and victory are brought to Christians through adherence to God's Word. Jesus' shed blood defeats Satan's power so that Christians truly experience life in His abundance.

Aquarius: After Jesus had ascended to the Father, He sent "The Comforter," His Holy Spirit Who is seen in this "Outpouring." Filled with power and might, Christians who drink of the Spirit are overcomers in every area of their lives.

Pisces: The Lamb holds two Churches in his hand: the Old and New Testament Churches. Here, the New Testament Church breaks free of tradition and bondage to walk in the Spirit. The devil cannot keep the Church down, although it is not popular to the world.

Aries: Jesus, portrayed as the **Breaker,** came to set us free and to break Satan's power over His people forever. His long-awaited return ushers in the Marriage Supper of the Lamb.

3. His Final Plan

Taurus: Jesus returns in glory with the saints, pouring God's wrath upon Satan. To the Christians, Jesus is known as the "Good Shepherd" Who protects and tends His flock.

Gemini: Jesus and the Church are shown as one together. Satan is shown fleeing, for he well knows the power of unity between Jesus and every member of His Body.

Cancer: Christians are symbolized as shellfish who shed their mortality to become as Jesus is. They are guided to a safe harbor where they rest secure in Him. Also, the Jews return to the sheepfold.

Leo: Jesus is symbolized as the Lion of the tribe of Judah Who was prophesied thousands of years ago. God's wrath is ready to tip over on Satan, and God's bird of punishment prepares to finish the job.

Receive Jesus Christ as Lord and Savior of Your Life.

The Bible says, "That if thou shalt confess with thy mouth the Lord Jesus, and shalt believe in thine heart that God hath raised him from the dead, thou shalt be saved. For with the heart man believeth unto righteousness; and with the mouth confession is made unto salvation" (Romans 10:9,10).

To receive Jesus Christ as Lord and Savior of your life, sincerely pray this prayer from your heart:

Dear Jesus,

I believe that You died for me and that You rose again on the third day. I confess to You that I am a sinner and that I need Your love and forgiveness. Come into my life, forgive my sins, and give me eternal life. I confess You now as my Lord. Thank You for my salvation!

Signed _____

Date _____

Write to us.

We will send you information to help you with your new life in Christ.

Marilyn Hickey Ministries • P.O. Box 17340
Denver, CO 80217 • (303) 770-0400

MARILYN

HICKEY

BIBLE

COLLEGE

Explore your options and increase your knowledge of the Word at this unique college of higher learning for men and women of faith. The Marilyn Hickey Bible College offers **on-campus and correspondence courses** that give you the opportunity to learn from Marilyn Hickey and other great Bible scholars, who can help prepare you to be an effective minister of the gospel. Classes are available for both full- and part-time students.

For more information, complete the coupon below and send to

Marilyn Hickey Bible College
P.O. Box 17340
Denver, CO 80217
(303) 770-0400

Please print.

Name Mr. Mrs. Miss _____

Address_____

City_____ State _____ Zip _____

Phone (H) (   ) _____ (W) (   )_____

Prayer Requests

Let us join our faith with yours for your prayer needs. Fill out the coupon below and send to Marilyn Hickey Ministries P.O. Box 17340 Denver, CO 80217

Prayer Request _____

_____

_____

_____

_____

_____

Mr. & Mrs.
Mr.   Please print.
Name Miss
Mrs. _____

Address _____

City _____

State _____ Zip _____

Phone (H) ( ) _____

(W) ( ) _____

☐ If you want prayer immediately, call our Prayer Center at (303) 796-1333, Monday – Friday, 4:00 am – 9:30 pm (MT).

For Your Information

Free Monthly Magazine

☐ Please send me your free monthly magazine OUTPOURING (including daily devotionals, timely articles, and ministry updates)!

Tapes and Books

☐ Please send me Marilyn's latest product catalog.

Name Mr. & Mrs. / Miss / Mrs. / Mr. _____

Please Print

Address_____

City_____

State_____ Zip_____

Phone (H) (____) _____

(W) (____) _____

Mail to
Marilyn Hickey Ministries
P.O. Box 17340
Denver, CO 80217

BOOKS BY MARILYN HICKEY

A Cry for Miracles ($5.95)
Acts of the Holy Spirit ($7.95)
Angels All Around ($7.95)
Ask Marilyn ($8.95)
Be Healed ($8.95)
The Bible Can Change
    You ($12.95)
Break the Generation
    Curse ($7.95)
Daily Devotional ($5.95)
Dear Marilyn ($5.95)
Divorce Is Not the
    Answer ($4.95)
Especially for Today's
    Woman ($14.95)
Freedom From
    Bondages ($4.95)
Gift Wrapped Fruit ($2.00)
God's Covenant for Your
    Family ($5.95)

God's Rx for a Hurting Heart
    ($3.50)
How To Be a Mature Christian
    ($5.95)
Know Your Ministry ($3.50)
Maximize Your Day . . . God's Way
    ($7.95)
The Book of Revelation Comic
    Book ($3.00)
The Names of God ($7.95)
The No. 1 Key to Success—
    Meditation ($3.50)
Satan-Proof Your Home ($7.95)
Save the Family Promise Book
    ($14.95)
Signs in the Heavens ($5.95)
Your Miracle Source ($3.50)
Your Personality Workout ($5.95)
Your Total Health Handbook—
    Body • Soul • Spirit ($9.95)

MINI-BOOKS: 75¢ each
by Marilyn Hickey

Beat Tension
Bold Men Win
Bulldog Faith
Change Your Life
Children Who Hit the Mark
Conquering Setbacks
Experience Long Life
Fasting and Prayer
God's Benefit: Healing
God's Seven Keys to
    Make You Rich
Hold On to Your Dream
How To Become More
    Than a Conqueror
How To Win Friends
I Can Be Born Again and
    Spirit Filled

I Can Dare To Be an Achiever
Keys to Healing Rejection
The Power of the Blood
The Power of Forgiveness
Receiving Resurrection Power
Renew Your Mind
Solving Life's Problems
Speak the Word
Standing in the Gap
The Story of Esther
Tithes • Offerings • Alms •
    God's Plan for Blessing You
Winning Over Weight
Women of the Word